HALF
THE MAN I WAS
Marlowe Whitlow

Thanks for all your love and support

Marlowe Whitlow

Thanks for
all your love
and support
Mahalo

Half The Man I Was
By Marlowe D. Whitlow

Copyright © MMXVII

Lowe Lost It Publishing, Inc.

All rights reserved

No part of this book may be used or reproduced in any manner whatsoever without the written permission of the author and the publisher.

Edited by Debra Davis Humble

Photos by Wayne Baranowski for Wayba Productions LLC
www.wayba.com

Cover Design by: Sean Hicks of Gargoyle Creative Services & Design
gargoyleonline.com

ISBN Number: 978-0-692-80139-0

To order more copies of this book,
visit us at www.halfthemaniwas.com

DEDICATION

In memory of my grandmother

MAGNOLIA WHITOW

There will never be a more beautiful flower
than you were, in my eyes.

You were there for me my entire life,
always cheering me on, no matter what.

You made me the caring, loving person that I am
today. I will forever love you. I'm missing the
smile you gave me every time I saw you.

God truly has an angel in Heaven with you there.

I know that right now you are smiling down on me
and if you were here, you would be
telling me how proud of me you are.

R.I.P. BIG MOMMA

HALF THE MAN I WAS
This is a story about how one man
found his whole self by losing half of himself…

INTRODUCTION 11

CHAPTER ONE
"Working in the Fast Food Industry" 13

CHAPTER TWO
"From Chicken Man to Dope Man" 17

CHAPTER THREE
"Business Owner – Mr. Flashing Lights" 25

CHAPTER FOUR
"The Aha Moments" (Part A) 29

CHAPTER FOUR
"The REAL Deal" (Part B) 37

CHAPTER FIVE
"Life from a Different View" 43

CHAPTER SIX
"Understanding Who I Was and How I Was the Product" ... 51

CHAPTER SEVEN
"Lowe's Life Lessons" (Part A) 59

CHAPTER EIGHT
"Lowe's Life Lessons" (Part B) 71

CHAPTER NINE
"A Leap of Faith" 87

CHAPTER TEN
"The Wrap-Up" 101

Marlowe's Cheesy Garlic Kale Chips 109

One Last Thing 113

INTRODUCTION

This book is the account of my journey from being an almost 500-lb man to the man that I am today. Many of us live life thinking that most foods are good for us. The truth of the matter is, we need to make changes in our thinking and to understand that, over time, many things are not. We live in a world where the food industry sells items that may be tasty to our palettes, but bad for our health.

In this book, I will outline how I got to the point of almost self-destruction …from things I didn't care about to the things I didn't know. I will also reveal the not-so-pretty ventures such as stealing from an employer for years and becoming an extremely popular "street pharmaceutical rep" along the way. Fortunately, I've risen above these undesirable acts that would have destroyed not only me, but also my family.

There were countless ways that I tried to get healthy by using various diet plans. Many people who were a big part of my life tried to help me on my journey. The toughest part was getting to that halfway point. It needs to be understood that although at 240 pounds, I'm still overweight and have a long way to go. According to the Ideal Height and Weight Chart- Body Mass Index (BMI), a man of my height, 5'7", needs to be in the area of 180-190 lbs at most. My goal is to be in the range of 200-220 pounds.

You will soon see my lifestyle stages that got me to this overweight point. The mindset that was given to me when I was a kid, as most of us have today, is that we were young and we'd be able to burn off excess calories. In fact, most African-American children, I presume, had this same mindset.

It's what we affectionately referred to as "soul food", food for our souls. In our homes, soul food was considered to be something good for our bodies. It was the way our parents were fed and their parents before them, for many generations since slavery. Today, I believe it is just our American culture, no matter what race, to indulge in overeating and eating foods that are not good for optimum health. We HAVE to take a closer look at the things we are eating and how it is literally killing us. We must learn to EAT TO LIVE, not LIVE TO EAT!

01 Working in the Fast Food Industry

When I entered the world of fast foods, I wasn't obese, but larger than I should have been. Luckily for me, I was a people person and still am. I got a job at a nationally popular chicken restaurant in 1989. I was placed in the home of the #1 deep-fried chicken of that era. Talk about heaven! Those 13 herbs and spices...and flaky, delectable buttermilk biscuits!!! This experience played a huge part of my story that now, I realize, started my addiction to food. I will tell you more about those biscuits at the end of this chapter. Well, it's no secret that the one COOKING the food is the first one to TASTE it. As every batch came out of the oil, I HAD to make sure it was "safe for the customers". You see, back in the early 90's, there were not many cameras focused on the cooks so I ate chicken and biscuits pretty much throughout my shift.

A man who owned several franchises owned this particular store. This guy was so blind because he sure as hell was not paying close attention to what was going on in his restaurant. As I was sucking down pieces of chicken and extra buttered biscuits, it occurred to me that this was a learned behavior from home. As a child, it was my job to butter the biscuits for my family. And butter them, I DID! At work, I was slathering them with about a pound of butter, inside and on top. Of course, this only lead to more fat clogging up my arteries. I was not making regular sized biscuits, but XXL.

As I mentioned, the owner never knew what was happening, but I began to pay more attention to the people working the cash registers. Most of them were either my family members or friends from school. When I went to the front of the store to deliver freshly fried chicken, I noticed that the majority of them always had loose change on top of the register. I asked one of my cousins for the reason behind this. She told me that whenever anyone placed an order, the cashiers automatically knew the prices. For example, if a customer's order totaled $19.75 and he or she paid with a $20 bill, a quarter was handed back to the customer. Then the cashier would then pocket the $20 (without actually ringing up the sale). This was going on for a long time before I ever noticed it. You see, I was a good guy and had never done anything like this before. Once, as a kid, I was in the grocery store and took a lollipop without paying for it. My mom beat the brakes off me! And that ended my career of stealing anything until now. But since I wasn't on the register, I had to think of another way to "get a piece of the pie." It wasn't hard to come up with a plan because I was pretty smart when I wanted to be.

Being the cook, I knew that at the end of the night we were always able to take a few pieces of chicken home. The chicken would have been trashed anyway because of sanitation laws. During the last hour of my shift, I would drop another rack of chicken, knowing we would not sell it all. I started taking BUCKETS of chicken to the "Dope Boys" across the street and selling it to them. I boxed it up, and soon the demand got bigger This soon led to my new nickname, "Chicken Man". Word quickly spread around the entire hood that I was selling chicken as a side hustle. My "customers" got bolder with their demands because they were hungry even before I was done working my shift. The next thing I knew, I was now selling chicken out of the front and back door, over the counter, and through the drive-through window.

I was still frying the extra batches at the end of the night, but since so many guys were actually coming to the restaurant for pick-ups, I started taking the leftover chicken home. Now, I was eating it all of the time, at work AND at home. I tell these stories because I currently see how easily it is to be influenced by the people around you. Positively, or in my case, negatively, it didn't matter. If you hang around people who are doing bad things, chances are you'll end up doing the same thing. This was the start of where a good boy went bad…eating and illegally selling chicken all day, every day, which eventually led to a different life of crime.

You may remember that I previously mentioned a story about the buttermilk biscuits. See, I didn't forget! I look back at it now and just have to shake my head. One day, after work, my girlfriend (now my wife of 17 years) and I were eating some chicken and biscuits that I had brought home. As she took the last biscuit, we had a huge fight that got pretty ugly. So much so, that we broke up! Can you say there was a more serious problem if the breakup was over biscuits that I made all day, three to four times a week?

HALF THE MAN I WAS

From Chicken Man to Dope Man — 02

I will be the first to tell you that I was not some hardcore drug dealer, but I dealt with the best of them. There were many levels to this. You may ask why I am telling you about the intimacies of my life of crime in a book on my weight loss. Please, give me some time and you will eventually understand. I'm stating how I got there and these stories play a huge role in how I became a bigger ROLL!

During my time at this restaurant, I met a guy, another cook, who became a good friend. Please keep in mind that I didn't grow up learning to do bad things; my mom did teach me better. But the life of making extra money selling chicken soon led to a life of selling other things. Greed can do that to a person. I noticed that this guy always kept a big wad of cash. This was way more than "chicken money"! For months, I repeatedly asked him how he did it, to which he tried to keep me away from that life. But I was persistent. Of course, I was still a little "green", thinking he had some super game on selling cases of raw chicken. To this day, I believe that was just one of his hustles. However, finally, he introduced me to the drug game.

I didn't have the heart to stay in it full-time, but jumped in and out over the years. Dope man to working (legally) man… my first drug sale was crack cocaine. I can tell you that selling crack wasn't my favorite because I had a real problem about what it did to people. Also, cooking it was not something that I was good at doing. I wasted more than I was able to sell, so this hustle didn't last too long. It's like counting points in a diet, too much work! I hated how crack turned people into zombies, their eyes looking like glass. You could see right through them and once they got hooked, it seemed that they couldn't stop.

This was a time when we would sit outside in the projects and wait for customers to come to us. We used beepers to enter codes and see the amount of the drugs desired. Once, when I dropped off a "package", I was floored to see one my own family members there. Needless to say, I was more than upset that my friend didn't tell me that one of my relatives was a "crack head". Prior to this point, I had done some teenage drinking, but now, it just got real. I was 16 years old with a full face of hair, walking into liquor stores, buying whatever I wanted. This was also where my weight gain took an even larger turn to the next level.

I had a daily habit of drinking alcohol and eating huge amounts of fast food. As the days went by, we visited various restaurants, but a favorite spot was a popular place in my hometown. If you're from the Kankakee area, you KNOW what that meant. DEEP-FRIED GREATNESS! I loved their gyro meat, but the sauce was not my "thang". I asked about different condiments to put on the sandwich instead. Let's just say when you are drunk and fat, you'll think of weird things. This was the birth of the gyro with BBQ sauce smothering everything, including the fries. I don't know if my friends who own the restaurant will ever give me credit for this, but I designed one of their signature sandwiches.

One summer day, in my drunken state, I ordered a grilled cheese sandwich. I asked how much it would cost to add gyro meat on it. He told me that was never done before and charged me $1.00. For the next few months, that was my meal of choice. I will never forget when I walked in there and saw MY sandwich on the menu; the cost, not the usual $2.95, but a whopping $4.25! I was extremely upset because that was MY creation! They did, however, add a little more meat to it and today it is one of their bestsellers. Now, in 2016, you can get gyro meat added to any sandwich and even on French fries. I told the owner that he should rename the sandwich "The Fat-Mac" which was one of my old nicknames. He wouldn't do it though. But I really would like my "cut". Fat drunk people have no rights. I guess it's for the best because I really don't want to be known for creating something that would make people obese and unhealthy. My mission now is to help others fight obesity.

My next level of the dope game was selling marijuana, better know as "weed". This was my drug of choice. Again, I am not proud of my past life, but at least this drug made people happy and didn't make them sell their souls. Most of my customers were drug dealers and thugs anyway. I was only drugging them after they were drugging others. I considered myself to be one of the best weed dealers because I took my time sorting out the sticks and seeds in order to have a quality product. This made loyal and repeat customers, a steady clientele, if you will.

Because of my prosperous "business", I didn't have time or really gave any thought to cooking meals. Fast food was it, and at this time, pizza became my choice. My friends and

I shared a house that soon became the party place. There was only furniture in one upstairs room. We partied on the first level and in the basement where Deejay Red set up his equipment. A keg of beer sat in the bathtub. We meant serious business, charging $5.00 at the door. Needless to say, we packed the house, especially since Kankakee didn't really have a night life to speak of for people under the age of 21. After paying the deejay and splitting the pot, we'd head to Denny's. Eating, sleeping, drinking, and dealing drugs was my entire life. Do I need to tell you how this had a major effect on my ever-growing body? Digestion was out of the question! Most people believe that smoking weed causes "the munchies"! This was something that I did for YEARS! It's no wonder that I weighed in at almost 500 pounds.

Now, on to the last level of my dope game…I wasn't sure if I would include these stories in this book, but if there is ever a movie, it will definitely be in it. I started dealing cocaine and weed with a high school friend who sold by the weight. After my many half pound purchases, he suggested buying them by the pound. I didn't have enough money, but being the smart businessman that he was, he gave me the extra weed and cocaine. Needless to say, my sales took off. The selling of one pound became five, five became ten and before you knew it, I was rolling in dough. I started buying houses and became a landlord, even buying myself one. Deep down inside, I knew that this was not God's plan for my life. My mother had "planted better seeds" in me. Everything I had was acquired in the wrong way; still, I was living it up. I went out to eat lunch with one of my best friends I.C. Dre every day…Red Lobster's seafood, dripping in butter…Chinese buffets, eating crab legs with more butter…

Looking back on that time in my life, I will say that I was lucky, no, I take that back, BLESSED, to have escaped death or prison. However, there was an incident where I was able to escape both. One of my "workers" called and came to my firstborn son's mother's house. He said that he had some money for me. When I went outside to meet him, a guy that was with him pulled out a 357 hand gun and held it to my head, demanding all of my money. I could tell that both of them were "higher than kites". One of the guys patted me down and took the few hundred dollars that I had in my back pocket. Now, like most guys who sold drugs, I always separated my money so I had several thousand dollars in my front pocket. The intent was to use this money to give to my supplier to purchase more drugs. Since they were so high and probably intoxicated, they didn't even feel that money. As they were running away, I ran for cover just as the guy with the gun let off a shot, which just missed me! After I had calmed down a bit, I went outside to discover that the bullet landed right at the level of my head. This was truly an eye opener for me.

Shortly after my last daughter was born, I was still in the drug "game". I often thought about what I was doing and what would happen if I got caught. I wouldn't be there for her or the rest of my family. My wife had been begging me to get a legitimate job and off the streets before it was too late. On one particular "date night", I got a text message from one of my customers. He needed a fix, or rather he had to "set someone up" in order for him to get out of going to jail himself. I was that someone. On my way to our meeting place, I was pulled over by the police for playing loud music. The funny thing about this was that I was in a rented truck, and at that time, the sound systems in rented vehicles were not particularly loud. I knew that this was the day I was about to "go down" for my acts. Needless to say, I had some drug packages on me, along with a two-way pager, a cell phone full of clients' numbers, and a pocket full of money.

The police put me in the back of their car and began to ask questions. They tried their best to get me to "roll the next big fish", however I was able to get past it and not give anyone up. I didn't want to become the next "rat" or as today's young people say, a "snitch". At this point, I began to think about the fact that my baby daughter was less than six months old. If I didn't cooperate and give the police any names, I might not see her for a long time. There were two brothers who were known around town for doing wrong to other people. Just as I was about to say their names, one of the officers told me not to tell them about these same two guys because they were already "working for them". Truth be told, besides the fear of not being able to raise my daughter, I was not built to be behind bars.

I had an uncle who worked at the jail and when he saw me being processed, he asked why I was there. I told him that I finally got caught up in my wrongdoings. About an hour later, he brought some "food". As I think back to this time, this had to be some of the worst food that I had ever had in my life! It was a dried out roast beef sandwich on some extremely hard bread. This was SO far from the lifestyle in which I had been living. I wasn't willing to eat that crap and thought I was going to die from starvation. However, the truth was, I had enough fat on my body to live at least another year.

That next morning, I was on the phone with one of my best friends who was also dealing drugs. I told him that I was going to die from eating crappy food and I needed him to bail me out immediately. He told me to wait it out until I got a bond reduction. My current bond was set at a whopping $75,000, of which $7,500 had to be paid upfront before I would be able to walk away. At this point, I was crying like a little girl, begging him to come and get me. Thankfully, I was out the next day. In less than 24 hours, I knew that I was "free" from the drug game and wouldn't ever be caught up in a situation like that ever again. The really sad part about this whole story is that I was more upset about the food, than the fact that I wasn't going to be free. Fat man's mindset…STILL.

Let's just say that the life of a drug dealer was not healthy for me (on so many levels). I was obese and all of my ill-gotten gains were eventually taken from me. I mentioned before that this life was not God's plan and I am convinced that He made sure I lost it all. God wants me to be a helper to people and not someone that hurts and destroys others. I believe He wants me to help on a bigger level. Many have done what I've done, but I'm willing to share my story with you, in hopes that it will change yours or someone's life from destruction by food.

HALF THE MAN I WAS

Business Owner – Mr. Flashing Lights 03

Now, this was a time in my life when I reached the heaviest weight ever. The biggest factor leading to this was my nightlife. As previously mentioned, I had always had some kind of hustle and it didn't stop after the "drug game" ended. I had always promised myself that if I had ever gotten caught, it would be the end for me. I'm so glad and grateful that I was able to come out of it without having to go to jail for over 24 hours or worse, prison. Even more so, that others could possibly learn from my mistakes while I'm still alive, rather than after my death.

After my brush with the law, I reluctantly went back into the (legally) working world. Let me just keep it real with you. I have and never will be the type of person to let someone else's dream be built off of my hard work, sweat, and tears. So, this phase didn't last too long. I had already given my life away to the working world for almost five years. First, I worked with the developmentally disabled for a year, and then became a driver of three years for a delivery company. I really loved this job because it allowed me to be active. Once I had learned my route, I was able to knock it out quickly and then sit down for hours and….EAT! Here's another reason that caused me to be an almost 500-pound man.

The next part of my "life journey" actually started in church. I have always liked taking pictures but never thought

I could get paid for it. After a friend, Bernice Watson, the unofficial "church photographer", loaned me one of her cameras, I began to do some pretty amazing things. Taking classes in graphic design led me to start a business called "Flashing Lights Photography". I started going around town to different parties asking if I could shoot pictures. Soon, I found out that the photographer had to pay the person in charge or the person that owned the building. In addition, I was responsible for providing the background scenery and props needed for every occasion. Since I was new to this and didn't have much money, I tried to buck the system.

One of the guys that I had managed while in the music game happened to be one of the biggest promoters in the Kankakee area. The "O-Boys" held the largest parties around. They wanted upfront money, but we were able to work it out where I took their pictures at no cost. This team worked well together and after a while, we were a force to be reckoned with. Before I came along, these guys were doing fine, but the way we put things together, made our team even greater! "Mr. Flashing Lights" (me) was born.

Business started off slowly, but picked up quite quickly. The word was getting around and the guys were organizing larger themed parties that took place once a month. Soon, it was four nights a week at a bar named Plush. Needless to say, I began going out to eat after every event plus consuming snacks all through the night. Business also grew because I was able to use social media as a tool to get the word out. People began to show up and OUT! 90% of the people in my news feed posted pictures that I had taken, either from the club or the studio. Suddenly, I was the outlet to see what had happened over the weekend in Kankakee.

This was great in the beginning, but soon it had its drawbacks. People were getting into fights over the pictures. Guys were taking pictures with women that they were not in a relationship with and vice versa. Now, I never wanted to keep up with who was "doing" who. I was working and making money. However, the biggest setback was that the pictures got the attention of my church family. Keep in mind; I was just at the club doing a job. However, the ladies started to bare more than a little skin and had me in hot water with the church. Women wanted to come to my studio and do nude pictures for their mates. Suddenly, church people were passing judgment on me, which my wife was not happy about it. I ALWAYS kept it clean, never any "wide opens" or touching. In addition, I asked them to bring someone with them, if possible. If my wife was free, I would ask her to be there as a safety net. This started a new rumor…my wife and I were sleeping with the people who were having their pictures taken. RIDICULOUS!

The "news" spread like wildfire around town. The proof was based on the fact that after I had a shoot with a particular young lady who "appeared" to be nude, she began to get calls from friends asking her if she had slept with us! Because she had nothing on her shoulders and from the way I had cropped the pictures, it may have looked like she was naked, but she wasn't. This made potential clients flock to me while others ran in the opposite direction. Regardless, business was booming and finally, we were able to take care of all of our bills, and of course we ate well.

The next three chapters will outline how I started to make changes in my life. I guess you can call this the time where I had my "aha moment".

HALF THE MAN I WAS

04 The Aha Moments (Part A)

At one point, my wife and I decided to try losing weight together. We both were able to shed 50 pounds, but her loss was more impressive than mine. Everyone could see hers, but mine was not as noticeable due to the fact that I was so big. It didn't look like I had lost any pounds. As people were talking about her transformation and not taking notice of mine, it did something to my ego. She was very happy about her weight loss and rightfully so. But, I will give it to her, because she made sure to give "props" to me for the pounds I had lost. She would tell people, "Marlowe has lost 50 pounds also". You should have seen the look on people's faces! All I saw was that big "caption cloud" over their heads with the words "Yeah, right"! Unfortunately, it wasn't enough to keep me motivated and I began to put on even more weight.

In the later part of 2012, I had been going to the gym consistently. This didn't include the countless years of making resolutions to get into better shape. Every year, I took a picture of myself and saved it on my computer to motivate myself to get into better shape, but THIS was the year I made a choice to stick with it. My first "aha moment" concerning my weight problem happened at my doctor's appointment. I had to make a change in my life before it was too late. I, like most people who are overweight, had to go to the doctor to get my prescriptions refilled. This was one of the two things that made me realize that something had to change. My doctor already had me on six medications. One was for the pain in my knees from being so heavy, two to control my high blood pressure and three for diabetes. But the most important thing that happened that day was the fact that he told me the next step was putting me on insulin. The pills that I took to control it were becoming less effective. I had been taking pills all of this time and now shots? This hit me like a ton of bricks! I had watched my grandmother do it for years and I knew that it was not something I wanted for my life. We can be told time and time again that we need to do something about our health, but it is not until a doctor tells us that we could die that we actually make the change. Most people would much rather try and fix the problem with meds before changing the way they eat.

The next thing that made me realize that I had to do something about my weight happened literally the next day. I had an event to attend which I needed to transport a lot of my equipment, so I asked one of my best friends Robert if I could use his truck to take the things I needed to the location. As a kid, I had always admired big trucks. This particular one was a 1989 Ford F 250 pickup and when I got into it, I was unable to drive it. My belly was touching the steering wheel; therefore I was unable to turn it. The next eye opening moment was when I went inside to ask him how to push the seat back. He told me that it was already back as far as it could go! To add more insult to this, I was unable to even fasten the seatbelt.

In November of that year, I had only lost about 20 or 30 pounds. At this point I created a group on social media called "MEATLESS FOR 30 DAYS". A friend of mine told me that his wife had tried it and lost about 40 pounds. Consequently, I made the choice to go without eating meat for 30 days starting on January 2, 2013. I just knew that I was going to get some help with this from my social media friends. I asked them to join me on this journey. Out of over 4000 people, only about 15 said that they would be willing to give it a try. New Year's came and I admit I was not really ready for this challenge, but since I had put it out there, I was not going to give up. I guess the fact that I knew I had told over 4,000 people I was going to do this and I was not willing to give up. This social media site has made and broken me in many ways. It kept me accountable because people were continually watching me on my journey.

I don't know how many of you watched "The Flintstones" on TV when you were younger, but there was an episode where the Food Anonymous guy followed Fred around, ripping everything he tried to eat from his mouth. I knew that people were watching me constantly, so I made a conscious effort to try to always eat healthily. I didn't want people in my face asking me questions like, "Are you eating meat?" or "Should you REALLY be eating that?" This took place at home most of the time. Going out to eat was "not on the menu". I was unable to find healthy choices so I did all of the cooking myself. I learned to try new things. My new meal plan consisted mostly of cheese, mushrooms, eggs, veggies and brown rice and I do mean a LOT of cheese. Dairy was my friend. I was able to learn how to eat new things and create meatless meals. I completed the 30 days; my days of eating red meat were pretty much over. During the next 30 days, I ate fish only and was able to lose 15 pounds during that time period. With hard work and a determined mind, I was down 25 additional pounds. I finished the month of March going meatless and had a 30 to 40 pound loss.

During the next few months, things did not move that fast (No pun intended). I was able to still workout at the gym but had slow weight loss. Over the next 5 months, I was only able to take off 10 additional pounds. This was not the speed I wanted. I would be on a roller coaster ride, going up and down 10 to 15 pounds. Needless to say, I was getting a bit upset with the way things were panning out, but I refused to give up this time. Over the years of trying various diets, I always started off with great excitement and hope. However, by March, it seemed as if I was plummeting down a slippery slope. This certainly was not the first time I tried to get my weight under control. I had tried Slim Fast, the Atkins Diet, and many other plans not worth talking about, but this year was different. I wasn't willing to give up!

I had talked to my doctor about gastric by-pass or lap band surgery sometime in June. However, I was on Medicaid and this procedure wasn't one that the state of Illinois was willing to pay for. My doctor told me that no one would even touch it. Looking back, I'm glad that I didn't pursue this any further. There are just too many limitations about what a person can eat after that surgery. This would have definitely ruined Thanksgiving, for example. The truth is, if making physical changes to the stomach and intestines just to help stop overeating, well, that's just over the top. So I left the doctor knowing it was not an option for me. Later, I did give the surgery more thought because I was now employed and my insurance would cover the cost. My doctor told me that I had to lose 75 pounds on my own before any surgeon would perform the procedure. The thought occurred to me that if I could change the way I ate and lost those pounds, why in the hell did I need to go under the knife? If anyone could make lifestyle changes and lose that type of weight before the surgery, why not just keep up the good work until the desired weight goal is reached? Now, I am SO glad that I didn't go through with this.

The side effects that followed this procedure were not something I wanted to deal with. If weight loss happens too quickly, the next procedure involves having the loose skin cut off. Trust me when I say that after losing over 240 pounds, things did not snap right back into place. This was a process and only time can fix the damage of living with that kind of excess weight on my body. I now understand that there are stages to this new way of taking control of my health and I'm willing to wait it out. I didn't get fat overnight so my skin wasn't going to revert back to its original shape so quickly. At the end of my weight loss journey, I may consider having this procedure done, especially if my doctor agrees that it is necessary for my well-being.

Around this time, I had communicated with a good friend, Roxanne, on social media. She was doing her thing with a weight loss program that I will leave unnamed. She was having great success and had lost a lot of weight. I called her because I knew I had started my walk into a healthy lifestyle before she did, and I wasn't willing to let her kick my butt with this. I asked questions about her program and asked her if she would share the info with me. She told me that this was a plan that she was paying for and if I wanted the information I was going to have to pay for it also. I told her that I didn't have the money to pay for the program. After a couple of weeks, Roxanne was willing to help me the best way she could and began to coach me. She inquired about my weight and told me to download a fitness app to my cell phone. I started tracking the food I was eating, counting my calories, and tracking the amount of food I was taking in for a couple of days. Now, I really learned the truth about the foods I was putting into my body. I was determined to stay under the calorie count she had given me, but the real factors here were that I needed to be aware of the fat, carbs and protein that I was consuming.

This is when I learned about macronutrients. There are three macronutrients that the human body needs in order to function properly: carbohydrates, protein, and fats. After I took a few days to enter my info into my fitness app, I was able to see where I was going wrong. I was taking in anywhere from 300 to 500 carbs, 150 to 200 grams of fat a day, and less than 50 grams of protein a day. This was way off the mark of where I needed to be. So, Roxanne took charge. She put me on 50 grams a day of fat, 150 carbs, and 140 proteins. This was a good thing for me, but I put in 1500 calories in the app and it changed some of my numbers of macros. I was only getting in 33 to 40 grams of fat a day. Since I was a novice user, I didn't pay close attention to the numbers to see that they had changed. A big shift in my body happened and I started to drop the weight very quickly. I started this new regimen on July 22, 2013, and after only a week, I was down 11 pounds. I got really excited about what was happening! I had already lost 35 to 40 pounds since January. So, to have lost 11 pounds in one week; I was on to something. I stayed with it for about 3 months.

Things were going pretty well as far as the weight loss was concerned. I was finally able to see some real weight loss. Ten pounds came off right away. By late September, I had lost between 22 to 25 pounds a month. At this time, I was home during the day, so I was able to cook most of my meals and counting/weighing everything that I put into my mouth. I kept a daily log of the numbers and was able to look at it every day to see my progression. Roxanne kept me on track everyday, asking me if I hit my target. At the end of every week I had to email her the final total.

Still, my mind held on to a few myths. This one is going to blow your mind. As I told you I had to hit my numbers daily. One late night, I called Roxanne and told her I was not going to make my goal. She said this wasn't acceptable and I had to hit the numbers in order for the program to work. There were about 80 grams of carbs plus 80 grams of protein that I needed to consume it was only about an hour before my bedtime.

Over the years of working on this weight loss, I was always told not to eat for 2 to 3 hours before bed. Needless to say, the "Drill Sergeant" Roxanne was on my butt to make it happen. I searched the cabinet looking at labels to find what I needed to make my goal. There I was, opening cans of tuna and looking for carbs without fat in them. I found some beans and it was on! Let's just say my wife wasn't too happy about the smell of things that night. Furthermore, I found out that sleep was extremely important and if I didn't get a full 6 to 8 hours, I wouldn't be successful on this journey. This also was a time in my life that I "took to the scale" every night before bed and again first thing the next morning. WARNING!!! This is not advisable to you. I did it because I was obsessed with my numbers.

I was sure that Roxanne had talked me into blowing my whole week with these shenanigans but I did it anyway. The next morning, after a full 7 or 8 hours of sleep, I went to the scale as I climbed aboard I was looking for some crazy number to be there but that was not the case. I had lost 2 pounds! This was so crazy I was thinking to myself; I know I passed gas a lot that night but did I have a bowel movement too? I cannot explain this but maybe some doctor can. When you sleep the body breaks down your food and I guess burns it off. (No bowel movement needed)

The next thing I learned while working with Roxanne had been something I was doing incorrectly during the early part of my workouts prior to her help. Cardio plays an extremely important role in the weight loss process. In order to get the best workout, it has to have some type of resistance. There must be some type of metabolic training involved. If you only want to lose weight and not build muscle, walking on a flat treadmill for an hour or two will only burn calories. I have learned that the best way to tap into your fat on any machine is to get that heart rate up and then take it down, up and then down…in repetitions. You can start off with short bursts of speed until you get up to a minute or two. When I first started doing this, I would do 15 to 20 seconds as fast as I could, then I would slow it down for 45 to 60 seconds. I swear there were times I thought my heart was going to jump out of my chest. If, for some reason, you can't do it that way, start doing uphill walks, setting the incline up as high as you can so you can feel the burn.

04 The REAL Deal (Part B)

Now, let's talk just a bit about some of the things I learned while on this program. In the beginning, I was cool with the guidelines and will never take anything away from its regimen because it worked. It was just very time consuming for me. Therefore, if time is something that you have on your side, this plan is for you. During this time, I ate some things that I won't eat anymore; well, let me say, that I will not eat as MUCH anymore i.e. red meat, fat free, or sugar free foods. I still, to this day, get pressured by friends to eat rib tips during the 4th of July season. There are just too many BBQ's and they know how much I love them. At this point, I become "Pookie" from "New Jack City". The rib tips just keep calling and calling my name! In the months of June and July, I always fall off of the proverbial wagon. It is my ultimate goal, to one day, be completely meat-free but for now, God is still working on me.

Here, I have to explain the terms "fat free" and "sugar free". As we all should know, if a food has sugar removed, another ingredient, such as fat, has been added that could possibly be even more unhealthy for the body. According to the Food & Drug Administration (FDA) and the US Department of Agriculture (USDA), "fat-free" foods must have less than .5 grams of fat per serving to use that label. Sounds good, except many of those foods can be higher in carbs than the full-fat versions and contain almost as many calories. Why?

Food manufacturers tend to add other fillers and chemicals (like sugar, flour, thickeners, and salt) to make up for the lack of taste, nutrients, texture, and palatability.

During my time on this program, I found a "friend" that I later found out was really NOT my friend in the end, OR a friend to my rear end. FAT FREE PRINGLES! I used to have a great love for chips. But as we all should know, they are full of fat. When I found them in a store, I had to have as many cans in various flavors. As the days went on, I started to have very greasy bowel movements. At the time, I didn't know what was going on. Fortunately, another good friend was paying attention to my weight loss and following my diet on my fitness pal. She loved to discover new things to eat as I did. But unlike her, I didn't research anything I was eating. Oh, but thank God she did! She noticed on the can that these chips were made with Olean. This product contains Olestra, which may cause abdominal cramping and loose stools. These symptoms, normally occurring only by excessive consumption in a short period of time, are known as steatorrhea, and are caused by an excess of fat in stool. Talk about a greasy booty! This reminds me of another pill that a doctor once put me on to lose weight. This man told me that the pill was new and I could still eat whatever I wanted to and still lose the weight. What he didn't tell me is that if I ate fried foods, I would leak like an oil pan without the plug. I read some years later, that this pill was pulled from the market for causing multiple deaths. Now, I try to stay away from all foods marked "fat free".

Since I was diabetic, sugar free foods and sugar substitutes were a way of life for me. I had been warned about using them for many years. Once, when out to dinner, my aunt told me to stop using them and that they were bad news. However, since I had used them for years, I was unwilling to hear her advice. But here is the ugly truth. There are few health concerns associated with sugar alcohols. When eaten in large amounts, usually more than 50 grams, but sometimes as little as 10 grams, sugar alcohols can have a laxative effect, causing bloating, intestinal gas and diarrhea. Product labels may carry a warning about this potential laxative effect. All artificial sweeteners are not created equally. Some will take a lot more usage for it to cause any bodily harm, but it's best not to use over a long time. The truth is, most of them have substances in them that, over years, have been found to cause cancer. Once I stopped using them, I noticed that "things" became more solid in the restroom. With the information I now know about whole foods, there are some things that I would have done differently.

Sorry to say, I didn't think I was going to be able to continue this program for the rest of my life. There were times when I was sitting down with my family and I was thinking, "Hold on a minute, I have to weigh my meat". I remember one particular day when I told them to wait until I weighed my chicken. My wife stated, "We are ready to eat now and don't have time to wait for you to weigh your food!" Consequently, I had to start doing things differently, making sure I had all my preps done before I called them to the table. This was a big part of my weight loss for this year; but after a few months, things slowed down. The next month, I was stuck at the same weight. This may have been just my body, but I think that after a while, my body figures out what I'm doing and puts up a fight. Quite possibly, yours does the same thing.

In 2013, I had set a goal to lose 100 pounds and was down 80 pounds at the beginning of November. With only 20 more pounds to go, the whole process came to a standstill. I knew that the holidays were going to make it rough but I wasn't ready to give up on my 100-pound weight loss goal. Here, let me be clear; I'm not saying that I couldn't have pulled it off with this program, but at this point, I wasn't willing to take a chance and possibly fail. This led me to the next phase of my weight loss and also a change in my mindset. Before we get into the next phase of my life, I have to make sure that I let you know I was extremely grateful for every step taken to get me to that present state. The regimen helped me to be more aware of the amounts of foods I was putting into my body (fats, carbs and proteins). This also gave me a better understanding of serving sizes.

So many people do not pay attention to them and it costs them in the end. Labels are marked for a reason and if you're not reading them closely, your body will let you know. Let's just take nuts for an example. Many times we hear that they are a great protein source and full of fiber, but what you have to understand is that this is for ONE serving per day. This means a small handful because nuts are loaded with fat. Now, don't you worry. In the words of the late Michael Jackson, "You are not alone!" I made the same mistake, eating bags of nuts daily. Back in the day, my best friend Marcus always asked me, "Why are you eating all of those fat pills?" Not understanding or paying him any attention, I continued to eat bag after bag. Let's just do the math. In most cases, depending on the type of nuts, a bag can contain 4-6 servings. Furthermore, they can have anywhere from 14 to 17 grams of fat PER serving, and that's just the unflavored ones. Today, there are numerous varieties available such as jalapeño and honey roasted, or may I dare say, "high fructose, buttery-dipped corn syrup"? Realistically, most people will eat the entire bag. As soon as it was opened, it was a wrap! Unfortunately, 102 grams of fat have just been consumed. Let me be up front or truthful with you; that isn't smart snacking at all.

HALF THE MAN I WAS

05 Life from a Different View

In November 2013, one of my mentor and now good friend, Sadeek, showed up in my life with a plan called the "90-day Challenge". By this time, I had built a following of people watching what I was doing with my weight loss. Sadeek, who lives in Chicago, was walking the streets of Kankakee talking to people about this challenge. By chance, or maybe divine intervention (if you are a believer), he walked into a business where my friend, Gary, was. He told Sadeek that I was the local man to talk to about weight loss. Getting the phone number, we scheduled a meeting. I have to tell you that THIS was a MAJOR turning point in my life. Not just because of the weight loss part of it, but now I was about to be a part of a community of people who have nothing but positive mindsets and endless, unconditional support.

At this time, I have to keep it real! I had already lost almost 200 pounds on my own so I really wasn't truly buying into the program at the moment. However, I told Roxanne that I was going to give this program a try. My plan was to mix the programs together, hopefully keeping true to my numbers. She was not happy and told me that I had to make a choice; I could not do both. Truth is, I'm so glad I had an open mind and was willing to hear him out. He was able to give me samples of the products and after tasting the crunch cereal… it was love at first bite!

I gave it a go and was able to lose 21 pounds in 12 days after being stuck for about a month. Now, I know that was a lot to lose in a short amount of time. This was the process for me with every new program I started. Things slowed down to an even pace after that. Over the next 330 days, I was able to lose 70+ pounds on this program. On the day before Thanksgiving that next year, I hit my low of 233 pounds! Oh, HAPPY DAY!!! I can remember it well. I was shopping with my family and I tried on a pair of pants, size 34. This was one of the greatest feelings that I'd had in a long while. I was back in the size that I wore in high school! I can say this about the program; it appeared to make a different shift in my weight loss. The inches were "inching" off my body. As excited as I was at this particular time, I was about to hit an all-time low point in my life.

My photography business was taking a nosedive. Things had slowed down "big time". I was still making appointments, but the money I made just barely covered the rent of $800/month. Most of the money that I made came from club parties and events. Unfortunately, our mayor shut these events down. There were fights breaking out almost every weekend. As I previously mentioned, the Kankakee area didn't and still doesn't have a "booming" nightlife. So many people, especially African Americans, were affected by this action. This was a crafty move on her part because selling alcohol was THE only thing needed to "keep the lights on and the doors open".

Even though I had a bar where I shot pictures every weekend, business was sill slow. Additionally, my wife had been laid off from her job. This made life financially difficult for us at the time. I had made a shift in my life to be healthier but the truth of the matter was that I wasn't doing very well. Just days before Thanksgiving, my car was repossessed. This act occurred right after we had received our 3rd eviction notice. I can laugh about it now, but I tell you, it was not funny that night. As with any couple having money problems, things were not going smoothly on the home front. We were fighting about almost everything. The "blame finger" was pointing heavily at me.

Since the business had been going downhill for some time now, my wife had been telling me that I needed to get a job but I wasn't listening. On the night that my car was repossessed, I had told her that I was hanging out with my cousin who was to pick me up. At some point, she looked out of the window and saw that my car was gone. As previously mentioned, we were definitely not on the best of terms with each other. Financial stress can certainly wreak havoc on a marriage! Consequently, she called talking frantically about my absence and about my missing automobile; so, my cousin took me back home.

Surely enough, when I got there, the car was gone. I was fully aware that I hadn't paid the car note in months but I thought if the "repo man" didn't know exactly where a certain car was parked, then he wouldn't be able to locate it. This is SO not true. Creditors hire individuals to ride around looking for these cars, and in time, they had found me. I did as any person would do when his or her car is missing. I called the police to report it stolen, but they already knew that my car had been repossessed. Regardless, I carried on with my night anyway, although I was "messed up in the head" and upset. My cousin and I still went out and he told me everything was going to work itself out.

Even though I was at a great point in my life, health wise, I just couldn't see any "light at the end of the tunnel". As the bills mounted, so did the tension in our home. At this point, I reached out to a longtime friend for advice and possibly a source of help. She was the accountant at the church where I was a member. She told me how some churches have emergency funds to help their members in hard times, but I would have to fill out some paperwork to get it. I did, and two days later, I had the money to get my car back.

Soon after, my life took a short turn for the better. After two weeks of meeting with Sadeek, he was able to share with me how I could help others on 90-day Challenge. He explained how I could share the elements of the program with others to help them lose weight also. This plan won me over for a few reasons. One, being that I did not have to count, weigh, or measure my food anymore. This was easy to do. I ate a bowl of super protein cereal for breakfast. For lunch I would make a nice well-balanced meal. Most the time it was a nice serving of lean meat and plate full of veggies. Sometimes I would add a serving of beans or low carb noodles. For dinner, I would make a shake from the program. This was not the order it had to be done according to the plan, but it was how I did it. Another reason for liking this regimen was the company's kids' program component. At that time, for every 10 pounds that I could lose I would be able to donate 30 meals to kids in my community. The program has since changed and now, for every ten pounds a person can lose, 90 meals are donated. The last incentive about this program was that if I could get 3 other people to follow it with me in the same month, I could get my meals at no cost.

However, the truth was, I was still on hard times and I couldn't come up with the money to order my first kit at the cost of $99. So, I told Sadeek there was no way at this time I could afford to make a commitment. Luckily for me, this was his time to pay it forward so he gave me the money to order my first kit. He told me that he would show me how to share this with others so I wouldn't have to ever pay for it, out of pocket. I placed my order for the monthly auto-ship, but made it very clear that if I didn't have 3 people before the end of the month, I was going to end my order. So I began to set up what was called challenge parties and invited others to come out and sample the shakes and cereal. Unfortunately, just before I started my first 90-day challenge, we were hit with another eviction notice. But, thank GOD for favor!

On that Sunday, December 1, 2013, two things happened. One, I started my challenge and two, God poured down a blessing. During the church service, the pastor told the congregation that there was a family who was going through hard times. He asked my family to come to the front of the church where he encouraged everyone to come up to bless us monetarily. I never expected that kind of support from so many people. It was enough to get us caught up, but the trouble was going to catch back up to us soon. After that, there were a few family members that stepped up to the plate to help us out. The largest supporter was my mother who shelled out thousands of dollars to help us with rent and bills. I am forever grateful to everyone who helped us in one way or another.

As I previously stated, during my first 12 days on the challenge, I lost 21 pounds. I went out sharing the program with anybody who would listen to me. It was a no-brainer from that point on. So on December 14th, I had my first challenge party, which delivered a great turn out. I decided that day to become a promoter for the company. This was a new start on life; I was able to help people in a way that wasn't as hard as my weight loss journey began.

The one thing I made very clear to my mentor was that I would not try and mislead people to believe that I had lost my first 170- 180 lbs. with this challenge. I never used my "before" picture with any ads without making sure everyone knew that my weight loss success didn't come specifically from that program. I just simply told my story. I let everyone know that it was, by far, the easiest method out of all the ways I had tried previously. This program also shifted the way my weight loss progressed. I wasn't just losing weight; I was losing inches in a major way! See, this program is based on NUTRITION, not DEPRIVATION, so my body started to "lean out" in a major way. Many people looked at the plan and saw how easy it was. But, as with anything going positively in one's life, there will always be a few "haters".

Many folks, to this day, will still argue about meal replacements; but the truth is, that it is just one way of life. Countless people live their lives on the run and don't have or make the time to prepare and consume proper meals. The Challenge program gives people the nutrition needed to start or end their days. Ok, I have to be realistic about this; numerous overweight people are eating "fat burgers" and drinking milkshakes daily. However, if given a shake that tastes like a Dairy Queen blizzard and they can lose weight from drinking it, chances are they would have a better ability to get on the right track to good health. Everyone has to find his or her way. Merely telling people who are 100 or more pounds overweight, to eat veggies and grains all day, in most cases, will not work. But if someone could find a way to get them started they soon will become addicted to the results and will find a way to keep going.

I'm extremely happy that I was able to get hundreds of people to this the plan. Many people were successful with it, but some were not. The truth is, there are so many ways to lose the weight, but until a person has made up his or her mind to make a commitment, it's all a wash. Until then, the unhealthy habits will continue.

HALF THE MAN I WAS

06 Understanding Who I Was and How I Was the Product

On April 7, 2014, I walked into the Kalmese Wellness Studio and met the trainer/owner named Kris Kalmese. At this point, I had lost over 200 pounds but needed to do something new to "shock" my body. A friend had previously told me about this center, so I went with the intent to just take a look around. Immediately, I noticed there was something totally different about it. I had been going to various gyms, using machines for my workouts. They worked for me because I was motivated to get and keep the weight off.

This day was like any other; I was dressed in workout clothes and ready for a WORKOUT. In hindsight, I wasn't prepared for what I was about to be put through. I told Kris that my friend and I were only coming by to take a "look-see". I vividly remember this day that changed my life. I was a little confused because there weren't many machines present. So I asked him about it and he stated that he used mostly body weight exercises with some weight lifting and cardio. As previously stated, I only wanted to look but HE had something else in mind. Although I told him that we had another appointment soon, he asked me to give him 5 minutes. Little did I know, that these five minutes were going to be the start of a great friendship with a great mentor.

Before I could blink twice, Kris put me on a leg press, loading multiple plates on it. Then he placed 30-pound dumbbells in my hands. As I told you before, I had been working out at other gyms but I never had a trainer. Before this workout, I was under the impression that I was in pretty good shape, but this routine proved me wrong. I pressed with the weights on my legs and arms and not even 2 minutes into it, I was praying…no BEGGING God for mercy! The pain was so real; the burn was something that I had never felt before. I literally had to crawl out of the machine when it was over. (Almost in tears, I might add) The great thing about it was my friend recorded the whole act on his phone and posted it on the most popular social media site. Consequently, I'll be able to go back and take a look at these 5 minutes of pain over and over again.

I returned the next day to talk to Kris about working with me. God again put another angel in my life. Kris told me the cost for training and my face hit the floor! Not because the value wasn't there, but because I had no way of coming up with that kind of money at the time. With my income from the studio and the fact that I wasn't doing very well with my networking business, I was barely able to pay my household bills. I told him that I couldn't afford it. So, we made a deal. Since I had over 5000 friends and followers on social media, I told him I would share my story with them and would work to get as many people as I could to join the wellness center. From this point on, I began to share videos of our training sessions. At this moment, I won't say that he didn't already have a growing business, because he certainly did. I'm positively sure that he would have continued to grow without me. As a result of my social media video posts, many people were intrigued and came to the gym to check it out.

These were some of the best times in my life. I now had someone who was going to push me and make sure that I was giving my workouts my all. I woke every morning, excited to work with Kris. He was able to get me to do exercises that I never would have even dared to try before. As time passed, I was trying things like hand and headstands. Now THIS was just unreal to me! Can you even imagine me trying to do these at almost 500 pounds? The training that I was getting excelled what had been happening with me since starting the challenge. Let me explain. Since I started using the products from the program, my body started to lose more inches than pounds. The plan had a more nutrition-based approach where I was taking in more protein and fiber as opposed to the other regimens. At times, it was a little difficult for Kris and me to agree on some things, but we didn't allow it to get in the way of us working together. My success was partly his success; we were a team.

Kris is a holistic diet type of guy, so he didn't believe in meal replacement shakes and cereals. However, I continued to use it as part of my diet to get protein and nutrients in my body. I still believe that meal replacements are a great way to get some of the important nutrients that a healthy body needs. Today's food just isn't what it used to be. The amounts of chemicals that are being used for food growth and preservation are killing us, literally. I must say that he did introduce me to quite a few new things that have great nutritional value such as wheat grass, chia seeds, kale and many exotic fruits. But keep in mind; Kris had never been a 500-hundred pound man before. I say this to explain that until a person has been obese or morbidly obese, he or she wouldn't understand trying to encourage someone to eat only food items from the earth such as wheat grass. It just wouldn't work in my opinion. Introducing an overweight person to a shake that tasted like something from Dairy Queen would probably fare better. I can tell you from experience, if, when I was almost 500 pounds someone told me to eat kale and wheat grass… I wasn't having it!

As Kris and I had more conversations, I learned additional information about meat and why people shouldn't let it be a big part of their diets. I stopped eating it as I continued working with him. He and Sadeek, also a non-meat eater, shared how meat was processed and the effects it has on our bodies. I also learned how eating red meat might lead to cancer cell growth, although researchers aren't 100% sure. I suggest that you investigate this for yourself. There are many documentaries sharing data about the food industry and all the harmful things being done. It would possibly scare you meatless if you watch them. Even fish and chicken, among many other animals, are being injected with so many hormones and steroids in order to grow rapidly for our consumption.

Therefore, I removed meat from my diet again. This wasn't too hard for me to do, but I do eat fish occasionally.

I started cooking once again and this time, the Internet made it a little bit easier. I was able to find various kinds of food to prepare. Of course, I was posting pictures on social media and it was good stuff! People started sending me messages asking for the recipes, but the truth was, half of the time, I didn't know what I was using to create these dishes. I would look at the recipes online and when I didn't have what was called for, I would just pull something out the cabinet and just start shaking it in. If I have to say so myself, I made some very tasty dishes. In hindsight, I wish I had written them down. Who knows? There could have been an entire cookbook in the making…Marlowe's Meatless Masterpiece Meals perhaps?

Kris's regimen was more on the side of strength training with lots of cardio. Now, I was running wearing weights or I was on a treadmill with the incline at its highest level. I loved the pain he put me through. It's like the saying goes "no pain no gain". However, I felt badly about not having money to pay him. The small earnings from my business and networking left very little after taking care of the studio rent and household bills. Furthermore, there were times when I traveled to out-of-state trainings. I often wondered how Kris felt about that. He's a really good guy and I believe he just wanted to help me continue to be successful on this healthy journey. My wife, on the other hand, was not happy about these trips and couldn't understand how I always came up with the money.

Let me refresh your memory. Do you remember when I talked about my life as a drug dealer? Well, over the years, I was able to buy nice gold and diamond jewelry. One year, there was a national training in Texas. My team wanted to make sure that everyone who wanted to attend would be able to go. A bus was chartered for this event. I took two huge diamond rings to a pawnshop to exchange for cash. One was worth $1200 and the other $1500, but you know how that goes. I was given less than $300 total for both of the rings, but I had to do it. It really wasn't a big deal to me because they were ill-gotten gains. My payday from the networking business was not until the day we were leaving and the bus had to be paid for prior. The very next trip came and again, my cash flow was short. I didn't tell my wife about the rings because I wasn't wearing them anyway. No one missed seeing me wearing them. However, when I prepared to go to Florida one year, I sold one of my 3 cameras to get the money to buy my plane ticket. My wife just could not understand it.

Again, I did make money from the networking business; it just wasn't enough to cover living expenses. There were months where I would bring in almost $2000 and then other months only $200. I just want everyone to know that the results you get depend on the time and energy you put into the plan. Networking is the most misunderstood business. Many people get into it thinking it's a "get rich quick" plan; when it doesn't work, they quit and become pessimistic. Well, the truth is, one has to put considerable time and energy into this type of business. If you don't work it, it won't work for you.

While working with Kris, I learned to believe that I could do anything I put my mind to. It wasn't just about the weight loss. He told me that it takes a strong mind and willpower to do what I had done on my own. Working with him taught me to push past limits and if I didn't do that, I would never know what I was capable of doing. I'm now able to accomplish things that I never would've even tried before. He also made sure that I understood that what I had done, I needed to understand that I was the product and that I would be able to help many people with my journey. Kris wanted to make sure that I understood that people follow other people who are doing real things. I also learned that the cost of eating healthy wasn't as costly as I thought. People like to say that they can't afford to eat healthy but I beg to differ. Anyone can take $20 and go to a store such as Aldi and eat great for a week. Meat doesn't have to be a part of your daily life. There are so many other things you can eat and get all the nutrients you need. Several varieties of protein sources are available for consumers. At this moment, I would be lying to you if I say that I never eat meat because sometimes I do eat fish, chicken, and turkey. Nowadays, pork and beef are pretty much off the table for me. I am known to "fall off the wagon" sometimes around "rib tips season" (4th of July). However, the cost of not eating healthily may be an XL wooden box. You have a choice to eat correctly for optimum health, or you can just keep eating from "the dollar menu" and your family will pay the cost of putting you in the ground sooner than expected.

HALF THE MAN I WAS

Lowe's Life Lessons (Part A) 07

At this point, life takes on a new meaning for me. Many lessons were learned over this journey about others and myself. The experience has made me a completely different man. In the first three chapters, I outlined how I got to be an almost 500- pound man. The following three chapters contained some of the things I had done to get healthier. In retrospect, I've never given any thought about these memories until I started writing this book. In the next few chapters, I will share some of the life lessons I learned and how they molded me into the man I am today.

When you have a transformation as I did, people and their perspectives change. I'm being totally honest with you. Yes, I've changed; but I think what I have accomplished was for the better. Sadly, not everyone sees it this way. Some people believe I am arrogant, but if they knew me before I lost the weight, I was the fattest confident guy around! For example, when asked, "How are you doing?", I would reply, "Fine, or at least that's what they tell me." (This reply really gets under my editor's skin.) But truth be told, I just wanted to do all that I could, to help as many people possible. It's no secret that I used social media as one of my biggest tools to share my story. Additionally, I started hosting workout groups. The support I received was awesome! Meeting with them gave me opportunities to challenge them to "pay it forward". Through my efforts and their cooperation, I was able to donate thousands of meals and snacks to kids in my community for every 10 pounds that my supporters lost. In addition, the networking company did a worldwide group workout, simultaneously, hoping to set a world record. On the local front, I hosted two events that day with 50+ people joining me in the gym. The best part was the 30 healthy meals and snacks donated to local children for each one of the 50+ participants.

As time passed, some folks wanted to be "in the closet" with his or her weight loss count, unwilling to share their results publicly. This action unfortunately slowed down progress, and in some cases, halted the meal donations. I'll be honest, this really upset me. All a person had to do was share their results with others and, they too, could get their food without cost every month. I went to countless local people trying to encourage them to become a part of the networking program. I truly felt that getting healthy and helping kids at the same time was an awesome deed. Churches, schools, daycares and gyms were my target places to visit. Just by sharing my results, I've been able to get my meals at no cost for over 2 years.

I don't want to make this about one company alone, but I need to make a general statement about the opportunities one can have with network marketing. For many years, this has been a great income source for those who are willing to stay committed to the process. Success doesn't happen overnight. Many of these companies have programs to help children and adults who are less fortunate; some have awesome compensation plans with great incentives i.e. bonus checks, paid vacations, high-end automobiles. Countless people have been able to supplement their income and or retire from their chosen professions.

When you change the way you live your life, sometimes the people in your life will change their attitudes towards you. I quickly learned this lesson, although at first, I was unable to see what was going on right in front of me. People were less likely to invite me to events where "unhealthy eating" was going to take place. Did they really expect me to shout through a blow horn, "STOP! Put that cheeseburger down!"? Maybe they thought I was judgmental. Once, I was invited to a birthday party where I was told, "You can just forget it! I'm going to eat whatever I want to eat!" What this person really didn't understand was, I'm not like that. I try to live my life by example, hoping other people would possibly learn to avoid the foods that I knew were detrimental to a healthy lifestyle. While everyone else was eating pizza, chicken wings, and cupcakes, I was eating a salad. I truly wasn't there to judge anyone; I simply wanted to fellowship with friends and family.

Furthermore, I learned that everything I said to certain people was taken the wrong way. Family members were unable to accept ANYTHING I said to them about food matters. Talk about hurting my feelings! They made me feel like I was coming down on them, never just me trying to help. Once, a family member told me that I think I was too good now, too "perfect". As you can probably guess, I wasn't the first one to get invited to the family or friends BBQ's. Most likely, many were thinking that I'd be standing over them watching everything they put in their mouths. I would've never done that, but if anyone had asked about particular foods, I would have been honest with my answers. Let me say this, I don't claim to know EVERYTHING about food, nutrients, the human body, and health issues. I'm just ONE man with a story to tell about MY weight loss experience. Just perhaps, someone who reads this book will be inspired to make changes to become healthier. And for God's sake, PLEASE check with your doctor before making major changes too quickly. After many debates with many people, some seem to think that they can just "work off" bad food choices. Excuse the incorrect grammar, It ain't gonna happen! I know because I tried it for many years. I went to the gym for hours, every day, running, jumping and lifting. Then, I headed straight to a buffet because I felt like I deserved it. This never worked for me and it won't for work anyone else either.

Here's a quick little story about a time when I tried to help a woman who was just starting her journey on the challenge program. On social media, she posted that she wanted to get a funnel cake and some homemade ice cream but didn't want to "mess up". A friend said that she would go with her to a local festival and they both could get one. Now, maybe I should've minded my own business, scrolling past without making a comment. But, oh NO! I wanted to be helpful and encouraging. What occurred next was pretty raw. I posted that I had a healthy recipe to make a shake that tasted like a funnel cake, one that she could share with her friend. I even volunteered to make it for the both of them. She took offense and "came at me" with a very vicious attack. She posted so much slander about me and didn't stop her rant for an hour! The one comment that I can remember was how she said that I "was just happy I could see my penis now". She had one thing right; I was incredibly happy to be able to see my lap! Of course, I apologized for offending her, which wasn't my intent. Now, I'll give advice if asked for, or I will give suggestions through a personal message. LESSON LEARNED!

That story leads me to my next point about watching others trying to eat healthy, but being afraid to say anything when I see it. Consider trail mix with dried fruit and nuts for instance. This misunderstood "healthy" snack needs additional explanation. Most trail mixes are LOADED with sugar! This comes from the way the fruit is dried and preserved with sugar. The nuts are full of fat and other ingredients are usually full of carbs. (PLEASE read food labels carefully, and "do the math".) It's okay to have a hand full when you need that pick me up, but let's be real. How many of us can stop after just one handful? I love a great mix myself, but I'm just like most people…once I open a bag that is it! It's a wrap! Now, here, I need to be really careful with this next statement because it can be highly debatable. Many people will fight over the idea that one could consume too much fruit. I'm just going to say it just like this; you have to know what your goal is and how you want to reach it. If you are trying to drop weight and you're taking in 200 grams of sugar in fruit alone, not to mention the other foods that you are eating throughout the day, chances are you won't be successful.

I feel there is a point where one can say that he or she has become somewhat a professional at something. There have been many times that I have wanted to help various family members, but for some reason, they chose to do something differently and worked with other people. After losing over 240 pounds, only to see the people that I love unwilling to take my advice was a bit hurtful. This made me take time out to think if I had the touch to be a blessing to others. One family member told me that when I talk to her about weight loss it made her want to go and eat a pack of Oreos. What sense does that make? Additionally, I had others pay dietitians to give them the same advice that I had been saying to them for years. THE EXACT SAME ADVICE. The only difference was that I didn't have the certificate or license on the wall. Everything I'd learned was from life experience. This is how I feel about the knowledge of personal actions versus book knowledge. Until one knows how a person who is 50-100 pounds overweight is feeling when you're telling them that you can't eat foods that you've been eating for years, you don't know SHIT!!! At this point in my life, I love how losing the weight has made me feel. Everything I posted on social media was about my joy and progress I had obtained.

Yet, still, all was not peaches and cream…especially on the home front. When I first started cooking, I wanted my family to eat the foods I was eating. This didn't go over well with my wife and my then, almost teenage daughter. Quinoa fritters and meatless dishes were not what they had in mind and the smell of my homemade kale chips caused a clash almost every time. This is funny now, because now I have to "fight" with my daughter about them. She loves them! This is weird because she usually won't eat any vegetables we serve, and if given a choice, she'd "plead the fifth". One night, I only made a small batch and didn't have any plans on sharing with her. So, I waited for her to go to bed. I quietly put the kale in the oven, but my plan didn't work because the smell was "loud"; the moment the aroma hit the air, she was UP! I mean, it was like she was a shark and someone was in the water bleeding! She stuck her head out the door and asked, "Is that kale I smell? What's unbelievable to me is that she wouldn't even try them any other time I wanted to share them. However, when her friend was visiting and I was cooking them and she asked to try them and loved them. From that point on, she has never turned her nose up at them.

There was a time when my wife said, "We (she and our daughter) like our food full-flavored!" In other words, she wanted meals with fat and carbs in them. So, when I cooked their food, I used oils and butter. I would use cooking sprays, free from fats and butter-flavored substitutes such as "I Can't Believe It Is Not Butter" in mine. Some of the items that I used to replace oils and butters, I later found out that they contain ingredients that I didn't want to consume anymore. At the time of this writing, my family now enjoys a few of the dishes that I created, which makes me feel good.

There were times when I would argue with my wife about some of the foods and the amounts of food that our youngest would eat. She was constantly consuming large amounts of carbs and sweets. Whenever I would say something about it, my wife would snap back, "You did the same thing when you were younger. She's young and has a high metabolism; plus, she's active during the day. She'll be ok." I guess the biggest mistake parents can make is believing that metabolism myth. I'm sure my mother was thinking the same thing when I was a kid. All of that macaroni and cheese, noodles, fried chicken, and let's not forget the Jiffy cornbread with the extra tablespoons of butter in the middle of it…well; you can see how that turned out for me. I pleaded with them to understand. But as the saying goes, "when you know better, you do better". My daughter heard us disagreeing, which wasn't a good thing. Everything I said fell on deaf ears. People have to come to the point where personal health is important to them, especially family members.

Another bone of contention was the act of dining out. There were times when we would fight over where we were going to go. Other than salads, there wasn't much on the menus that I would be able to eat and stick to my plan. My wife once told me that she hated going out to eat with me at all. I have to understand it from her point of view and now, thinking back, I can understand her frustration with me. At this particular time, my money still wasn't great. Wait! Let me reword that; I didn't have ANY money to pay the bill. But, I wasn't folding on this one with her, buffets were not in my best interest and I was determined to stay away from them.

It is truly hard to keep people on the right path or even to simultaneously get them on the same path as you. Even though I had a good track record and had done something that most people only dream about, it's still difficult to get people to listen to me.

Sometimes, it's funny to hear some people try to tell others what to do because they lost weight at one point in their life. (Try losing over 240 pounds and maintaining it for 2 plus years!) You have to be very careful when you talk to people. What worked for you may not work for them. I did some crazy things trying to stay on track. There were times when I would be in a restaurant and I would be full! However, I would take the top off of the shaker and pour salt all over the remaining food to prevent me from eating more! The fact that I was already full should have been enough to stop me from eating more but the truth was sometimes it wasn't. There aren't many people who you run into on a daily basis that can tell you what a 100-plus pound overweight person is thinking. I can tell you one thing that they are NOT thinking about… and that is when they can get their hands on that next leafy green salad. By the way, the extra salt thing did not work at the buffet because you could always just get a new plate of food. Too funny! Too real!

One family tradition that my wife and I had with our older children that we don't do much of with the youngest daughter was weekend movie nights. However, she did experience it a few times when I was 400-500 pounds. The reason I want to give this some attention is because there was a huge problem. I'm almost embarrassed to share this with you but since this book is all about truth, I must tell it. First, popcorn is something I TRULY have a problem with. Like summer time and rib tips, popcorn is another food item that I just get so weak around. The smell alone has my "Pookie" antenna going haywire! When my older children and I went to the movies, I had the money to get them their own bucket to share, and I had my own. Now, when my daughter and I go, the two of us can kill a bucket of popcorn before the movie even starts! Many people will say, "Hey! It's only popcorn; it's not that bad!" This is so far from the truth. First, it is a carb, and one you can eat a lot of without batting an eye. Secondly, the "butter" that movie theaters use is nothing but fat and may stop a heart in its tracks. The most embarrassing thing is when Baby Girl and I were eating the popcorn, I would get so mad that she was eating more than me! When I say mad, I'm talking fighting mad! I can laugh about it now, but the truth is, some family outings were ruined by my childish behavior. My wife had to constantly break us apart. What was really messed up about this was I would get sick to my stomach from the butter. Sometimes, so much so that I'd be in the bathroom puking up my guts. I really didn't understand. I knew this was going to happen every time. Some things are truly addicting; this was one of mine. I still can't resist popcorn when I go to the movies, but I can do without all of that butter.

Over the years, I had to learn not to say anything to my family about eating unless asked. The truth is that sometimes, I can be a jerk about it. It really bothered me when I would give advice and then they would take someone else's, only to come back to me with the same exact questions again. It makes no sense to PAY for professional advice when I could have given it to them at no cost. I have been told that I can be a little aggressive when I talk to family about getting healthy, but I just think that my passion is so strong; it's hard to understand sometimes.

Social media is a very powerful tool. In the last few years, I've learned a few do's and don'ts. For example, I try to stay away from topics on race, religion, politics, and sexuality. When you think about it, these four "hot buttons" are the basis of talk shows and tabloid magazines worldwide. They've also been known to divide families, relationships, and even countries. I have many people following me on these social media sites for various different reasons, which is why I've become very careful about what I post on my pages. There's always the possibility of losing followers who are seeking weight loss advice or tips that may be offended if I spoke my opinion on these topics. Many eyes are watching and you just never know when someone is going to take your words and "twist" them to fit their agenda. But here it is in a nutshell; I don't see "color" in people. We're all human beings. Religion, politics, and sexuality are personal and vary greatly. In my opinion, people have to make decisions about themselves based on their beliefs. That's all there is to it.

However, people who I expected to "have my back" have hurt my feelings. One day, my wife told me that one of her family members who happened to be a childhood friend of mine told her he was going to have to delete me because he was sick of seeing all of the positive $h!+ on his timeline. Wow! To think that someone wanted to delete me because I was being too positive was disturbing to me. I had already reached the limit of people that could be my "friends" and had been thinking about deleting some people anyway. Additionally, I had over 500 people on my friends request list. The only reason I didn't delete anyone was because I wasn't sure who was following me and why. If someone from my past followed me because of what I've done with my weight loss, I would miss that opportunity to inspire or motivate him or her. Consequently, I never deleted anyone for that reason.

HALF THE MAN I WAS

Lowe's Life Lessons (Part B) 08

Humility-a modest or low view of one's own importance; humbleness.

At this point in my life, I had to humble myself. I had depended on my photography and networking businesses to get me by in life. However, things had slowed down so much in both areas, that my back was "up against the wall". My wife was fed up; the timeline that she had given me to build an income enough to help support the family was long overdue. She had a good job with a pretty decent income, and all she wanted me to do was to help her. Because her salary was as much as what some couples made together, I felt like she could've "cut me some slack". I also felt that she owed me because I had taken care of the family for years. But she called it like it was. I had lost my hustle; I wasn't willing to get out there and make a way like I had done in the past. I used to do whatever I had to do to make money, i.e. selling drugs and bootleg movies, photographer and graphic designer, to name a few. But I had lost all of my drive to do any of those things. All I wanted to do was exercise and help as many people as I could to see the benefits of living a healthier lifestyle.

I lived like a king and looked damned good doing it, in my opinion. But inside, I was dying and feeling worthless to my family and all of the people around me. I had friends and family that would call and ask me to do things and I'd tell them that I didn't have money to do anything or go anywhere. Most of them would tell me that they didn't ask me if I had money. They simply wanted my company and would cover my cost without expecting repayment. On many occasions, my wife and I went to social events with cousins who were always treating us. Don't get me wrong, there were times where my wife was able to foot the bill, but most of the time it was on them because they wanted to do it. When I was hustling, I used to be the one paying, but because I used ill-gotten gains, I feel that God took all of it from me. I needed to pay for all the wrong I had done.

I felt like I had hit rock bottom. My wife took care of what needed to be done to maintain our home and I had a place to lay my head. However, it took me a long time to accept the fact that she just wanted me to feel like a man again. Because I couldn't pull money out of my pocket to buy anything, this realization started to wear me down mentally. How did I go from a man that once walked around with hundreds of dollars in his pocket and thousands at home in a safe to a man with no cash to call his own? Then my wife said these words, "You can go get a job at McDonald's". Oh, HELL no! I replied. Working in a fast food restaurant was one of the reasons I had been obese. This would have destroyed everything that I did to get to be half the man I was! This compared to putting a crack head in a crack house and then telling him not to smoke the crack. RIDICULOUS! I had changed the way I looked at food, but I was not willing to place myself in that kind of situation anymore.

I still don't know who's to blame for the fall of my photography business. It could've been the people who were gossiping about me around town. Or maybe it was because my weight loss success dominated all of my conversations. I was obsessed about it on my social media pages. Furthermore, since I was challenging my whole city to get healthy with me, more rumors started to generate. All I wanted to do was help people lose weight. But many people continued to tell me that they missed my photography work, and now had to hire other photographers. I heard this so much that it almost drove me crazy.

In August 2015, a friend offered me a job opportunity. Previously, I had shared my financial woes with him. He told me that he had some openings for temporary employees and that I could begin working as early as the next week. He made no guarantees about how long the assignment would last, but it would, at least be 4 to 6 months. I went to the temporary job service and filled out the necessary forms and took the required test. I was able to pass it and the drug screening. Meanwhile, the temp service sent me out on a one-day assignment at a school-daycare center to unload some trucks and put together all of the new equipment given through a grant. For some reason, I was given the leadership position for the day. Additionally, I was given the time cards for all of the workers. The people on that assignment were under the impression that I was the foreman. This job became the most humbling and humiliating experience in my life. It may seem as if I hated my friend for putting me through this, however it's not true. It was something I needed to push me into understanding what I wanted and needed to do with my life.

I was given the opportunity to work for one of the highest paying temporary jobs in my area and was told that it was a possibility that if I worked hard, I could get a full time position one day. Quite possibly, everyone may have been told the same thing, but I chose to believe that my life had taken a turn for the better. At least it felt great to be appreciated. Yet, I had to find a way to still get in my daily workout. My shift started at 6:15 A.M., Mon- Fri. So, actually, my day started at 4:00 in the morning in order to work out for an hour and a half. Fortunately, the gym was very close to the factory. When I started this job, I made it clear that I only wanted to work my 8 hours, 5 days a week and nothing more. I didn't take any of the overtime offered to me during that first month. As I was walking into the factory on the very first day, I saw an older man limping into the building. I couldn't help but think that working at this job had done this to him and I wasn't willing for the same thing to happen to me.

Even though I had made it clear to my supervisor, he asked me daily if I wanted to work overtime or at least, come in earlier. At first, I turned him down. Then I had an out-of-town event the next month with my network marketing business. I wanted to have a few extra dollars in my pocket so I agreed to work some extra hours. My next paycheck looked darned good after that, so I was "hooked" for a while. Finally, I started to see some "real" money and after spending so much time without it; I just couldn't stop. In the beginning, I had no problem working hard because I used the work as my personal workout sessions. There was a lot of heavy lifting so I was happy to be able to get some extra "health benefits". I learned how to run operations and how to test the product on the floor. Consequently, some of the "higher -ups" began to take notice. Then, I was told that two floor workers were going to be transferred to a different department. These spots were going to have to be filled. Even though I initially didn't want to work in a factory, I started to care more when my role changed from someone who just stacked and packed product. Learning how to make sure that all operations were running smoothly made my self worth rise.

My boss told me that the people who worked on the floor were either too young or not ones he would put in a leadership role. Shortly after, a pretty, young, Hispanic woman and I were being trained for one of these positions. She had started working there a few weeks before I was hired. I'm not saying that she wasn't a hard worker, but it did take more time for her to catch onto operations. The language barrier made it difficult for us to understand each other. Furthermore, she wore a pair of jeans that hugged every curve of her butt, and when I tell you that everyone was looking, men AND women, I'm not lying! It seemed as if she could do no wrong just because she was so pretty. I say this because one day, my supervisor told me just like that. He outright said that if she did anything incorrectly, people would run over to help her, but if I messed up, it would have me out the door because I was a black man.

Unfortunately, my relationship with my supervisor/friend who helped me get the job started to break down. Many people who knew him told me how he was difficult to work for, but I said that I had no problem working for him. This was all about to change and I mean in a very uncomfortable way. One day, he came and pulled me to the side and told me that someone said that he was showing me favoritism. He had to make sure he showed other workers that he wasn't. I wasn't sure what this meant but I never imagined how he treated me would change. This was a long time friend and a deacon at my church. Needless to say, I was no longer training for the floor position. This was a complete shock because I knew that the Hispanic woman was not doing a better job than I was.

Soon, more workers shared their personal stories about the way my "friend" treated them. They had never said anything to me before, in fear of me going back to "snitch". One thing I that I heard repeatedly was my supervisor was an "Uncle Tom". According to the Urban Dictionary, an "Uncle Tom" is a black man who will do anything to stay in good standing with "the white man" including betraying his own people. Even the Caucasian people in the factory were saying this! At this point, my whole demeanor and attitude changed, which everyone took notice.

Ironically, one worker, who happened to work on that temporary daycare assignment, told me that I had worked so hard when he was first hired and now I wasn't doing as much anymore. He didn't want to work with me. We started to get into arguments because of my unwillingness to work as hard. He didn't care about how he was getting treated and just wanted to keep moving. Honestly, after my supervisor told me that he had to make sure he wasn't treating me better than the other workers, he started acting like I was a "Hebrew slave"! After that, I didn't do a damn thing! I stayed in the restroom, on the phone making calls to solicit people to become a part of my business. I was doing everything I could to get my networking business back on track. I only worked just enough to prevent getting fired. The way he treated me in front of his boss, made me almost hate him.

Looking back, I feel this experience gave me that "kick in the rear end" to go to the next level. I started thinking more about life and what I really wanted to do with mine. Working in a factory was not it. My supervisor didn't like the person I had become. He had a look in his eyes that seemed to say, "Why did I recommend him for this job?" Well, since we had been close, he should have known that I was not the type of man to "lie down" and let people walk over me. He once told the temps that we couldn't go to the bathroom until break time. This wasn't going to work for me because I was drinking a gallon of water daily and green tea. I hadn't stopped living healthily. Furthermore, it got hot in that plant! I told him that I was not going to pee on myself; if I had to go, I was going. Sorry, slavery is over. My supervisor had no shame when I mentioned his mistreatment of me. As the person I had known him to be, I didn't expect him to say, "I can see how you can say that". He told me if anyone found out that we were friends, it would be harder for both of us. It really shouldn't matter if I was doing my job correctly. The fact that he was willing to train me for other positions told me that I had to be doing something right, but he continued to do things to make sure everyone see that he wasn't giving me any special treatment. I have many stories about my experience there, but I'm not sharing them all. I just wanted to make a point about the fact that no one mattered.

As you may already know, companies have a great knack of combining manpower with machine power. One day during a shift, the supervisors decided to run a speed test. I completely understand that some analyses have to be done in order to understand what works and what doesn't. It was strange that no one asked the people on the other side of the machine if this was something they could handle. The machine kicked out major footage and the people on the end were struggling. When I said something to the supervisor, he stated that if we couldn't keep up, we'd be replaced with other workers who could.

On the day I took that stand for everyone about the restroom privileges, I was placed in a position on the floor that required heavy lifting. The worker was to be rotated out after 4 hours. This didn't happen on that day. I was kept at this spot for the whole 8-hour shift. The next day I said it was unfair treatment, to which my supervisor replied he "forgot". That night, my wife said, "When on a job, you have to be quiet sometimes or you could end up doing things you don't want to do". So, the proverbial saying is true, "The squeaky wheel gets the oil!"

Things continued to spiral downhill. I had just started to get a few opportunities to speak at different health fairs and other events. I was becoming someone that was trusted to help others. However, my job made it difficult for me to do. I had already made it clear I didn't want to work any overtime. Therefore, if I had an event on a weekend, I would be able to attend. It seemed as if the bosses weren't happy unless the temps were unhappy. Every week, the supervisor would tell us that we would have to work on the weekend. Then, by the end of the week, things would change! "Suddenly" our weekend was free which made my schedule off balance. My picture was on an ad for a health fair, of sorts. However, that week everyone had to work because of a big job that had to be finished. I called the hosts of the event and told them I was being forced to work and wouldn't be able to make it. I had worked diligently to be able to have these opportunities to talk to people about a healthy lifestyle and my job was taking that away from me. On that Friday before the event, my supervisor told me that the full time employees had put in cards to work those extra hours; we weren't going to have to work on Saturday. I got on the phone as fast as I could to call the people from the event, only to hear that they had to fill the slot and I had been replaced already. I had to respect their decision; this was business and I had let them down a week before. This was yet another eye-opener to make me become more focused on what I wanted and needed to do.

The straw that finally broke the camel's back happened on a day where things got out of hand with my supervisor and me. The young woman that I was training with didn't want to drive or change the tank on the fork truck. So one day the tank on the truck was empty and she came to me and asked me if I could change it for her. I think I was enabling like everyone else. For some reason, I think she had the "damsel in distress' thing down pat. Me being the nice guy, I did it for her. On the way to change the tank, the truck stopped on me. This made me unable to get it back in time to be ready for the next load. About 20 minutes later, my supervisor pulled her to the side and asked her where I was. I was standing less than 20 feet away and heard him. I lost it in a blink of an eye! I started yelling across the room, telling him if he had questions about where I was, he should have asked me. So, there we were, in a shouting match on the floor. His bosses were in his office waiting on him for a meeting. He went into that meeting upset. I'm not sure if this was the reason that the so called "X" was on my back, but as soon as he was done meeting with them, he was right back on the floor to finish our conversation. I told him again how I felt about his treatment of me and again, all he said was, "I can see how you can feel that way".

A week or two later, I had myself together and was doing what I was being paid to do. I wasn't talking much to anyone but a young man that I called my "work son". There wasn't anyone else on the floor that I could trust, but "he had my back" and I had his. One day, I was the driver to take the product to the warehouse and I noticed that every time I turned a corner, my supervisor's boss was watching me. There had been other times when I would see him lurking, but this was different; this was creepy. Later that day, my supervisor called a meeting and told us to make sure that we were staying busy and keep moving because his boss was watching us. He also stated that some of us had "X's on our backs". I immediately pulled him to the side and told him that I knew I was being targeted. He shrugged his shoulders, put his head down, and walked away from me. But then, he later told my work son, "At least Marlowe knows that he has an "X" on his back".

I remember feeling like a deer being hunted. I called the temp service and asked if they could put me on a different job. I was told that their policy prohibited placing a person on a new job until the current one was finished. I put in my 3 weeks immediately and went back on the floor like nothing happened. I had had enough. On that same day, when the 2nd shift came in, I made sure that they knew which operations had been completed. I'm not sure what the 2nd shift supervisor was thinking, but he told my supervisor that I disturbed his shift meeting. This occurred on a Friday. The next day, my supervisor waited until the end of my shift to ask me why I stayed over to tell the 2nd shift what needed to be done. When I asked him why he wanted to know, he just smiled. I didn't find that funny and was hot. I felt like everyone was out to get me. I made a choice; I couldn't sit around and wait on the temp service to place me in another factory job. I will always remember this day as my leap of faith.

LOWE'S LIFE LESSONS (PART B)

On February 29, 2016, I took the day off. I knew deep down that my mission was helping people get healthy. I had been researching what it would take to become a personal trainer. After calculating the cost and time, I was ready to start my journey to better understand how my story could help others who were on the same path. I wanted to make sure I was making the right decision, so I went to the place where I spent most of my days working out…the local YMCA. I talked to a staff member that has been there since the beginning of my weight loss journey and asked her if they were hiring trainers. She stated they were, but I had to speak with the man who was hiring. After I put in my application, she told him my story how I started right there at the Y. Later, I spoke with him and told him how I wasn't certified, but I was looking to get the ball rolling towards certification. He explained to me that there was a woman who was an employee/trainer there who had lost over 100 pounds and was trained in house. So, I went on to the next gym. Because I wasn't certified, I was "shot down" at the door. In retrospect, I'm so glad that they didn't give me a chance because two months later the doors to that gym were closed for business. The last gym that I visited was not far from my house. I had never been there, but I made the choice to check it out and that turned out to be one of the best decisions in my life! The whole incident was different from past gym experiences. The only one other gym that I felt that welcomed was the Kalmese Wellness Studio. As I walked in the door, there was a guy standing there. He greeted me and made me feel welcomed. The pressure of walking into a place I'd never been before and talking to people who knew nothing about me was immediately released. The guy had on a name tag so I was able to address him by name. I told him how I wanted to do something to help people develop a healthier lifestyle. I told him that I want to train and that I had been looking into what it would take to become a personal trainer. He said they weren't hiring at the time but if I went online and filled out an application, he would get back to me if a position opened. Well, I wasn't willing to give up on this so I said something that I should lead with every time I talk to a person about health…MY STORY

I told him that I had lost 240 pounds and all I wanted to do was help others with the struggle of losing weight, making sure they understood that anything is possible. At this point, I saw the look on his face and that "We're not hiring" stance was gone! Immediately, I shared some of the things that I had done in the community to promote good health. I asked for his email address to send him some of my newspaper and magazine articles so he could see the "proof in the pudding". He gave me his card and asked me to send a "before and after" picture of myself with a resume. Furthermore, he said that their trainers were trained in-house with a program to get certification. Because I had put in my 3-week notice, I had no idea how I could make it happen but I had my mindset to find a way.

As soon as I got home, I emailed all of the documents he asked for, including pictures of my transformation. Then, I just happened to look at his business card and saw that he was the vice president of the company! This man was on the front line, dressed and working like he was just one of the employees. I was astounded! What happened next still surprises me. I sent that email at noon and by 1:45 P.M. I got an email from him telling me that he was very impressed while reading what I'd sent him. He asked me if I could come in on either

Wednesday afternoon or Thursday morning. I made the appointment to meet with him two days later after work.

Now, I had to have "the talk" with my wife. For some reason, I couldn't hold it back; I would no longer be employed in a few weeks. I told her about the conversation I had had with the temp service. However, she was already aware of their policy because she had been employed through the agency in the past. She took a deep breath and just stared at me. We had just worked on a budget together and had moved to a townhouse that was $200 more than what we had been paying. I told her I couldn't do the factory work anymore; I had to get out of there before I went crazy. The truth is, I think she went into shock at that moment because she had very little to say. But a couple of days later, that all changed.

We were lying in the bed and she jumped my bones and I do not mean in a sexual way. She pounced on top of me yelling, "What in the hell are we going to do now?" Grabbing me by my face, I could see she was almost in tears, but I also could see that it was more rage than anything. I think at this point, she was so angry she could've choked me out if she wanted to. I realized and understood that she hadn't planned on taking on this new expense by herself. And now, I had quit my job before I even had another one. In my mind, I wasn't going to let that factory job get the upper hand on me by ending my assignment unfavorably. So the moment it was confirmed that I was the one with the X on my back, I made that call to the temp agency without weighing in the consequences. I was so upset that particular day because I had been working diligently. If it had been one of those days where I was slacking off, I may have been able to deal with it better.

This has been my mindset for years; if a person is shooting, you go the other way and not run towards the line of fire.

I returned to work that next day with a new attitude. I did get the job at the gym and called the temp service to move my termination date up. The gym wanted me to start training as soon a possible. I returned to the factory and I was open about the fact that I was moving on to some of the people there. The fact that I was giving up one of the highest paid jobs in the town didn't make sense to some of them. I would never look down on the people who are willing to work in factories, but it just wasn't for me. Having to wear steel-toed boots, earplugs, and safety goggles all day was just something I didn't want to get accustomed to. The department that I worked in had very few windows and they were always dirty. Not being able to see what was going on outside wasn't the way I wanted to spend 8 to 12 hours of any day.

As I was leaving that place forever, a woman who had been working there for 20 or more years said two things to me that I just couldn't understand. She told me that this place wasn't a bad place to work at all. There is a lot of racism and they treat the temps like shit but besides that it is a great place to work. I just wondered if she was hearing what she just said to me. What was "great" about being treated like shit? I was done with her at that point.

I have no "bad blood" with my man, my supervisor/friend. I just know that I could never work with him again. I told him that this job was something I needed to humble myself. It truly set me on the right path to do what I loved to do and that was to help people. As my factory days came to an end he continued to say things that left me mystified. I don't even know how he could let them flow from his mouth. First, he said that I shouldn't have told anyone I was leaving because everyone was not happy for me. I never will forget how this made me feel. I had mixed emotions. First, I was pissed that these people weren't happy for me and I wanted to lash out at them. At the same time, I laughed at them for being so simple-minded. How could you not be happy for someone who was going to do something he loved for living? The last thing he said to me was, "You do know that the jobs that people love aren't always the ones that pay the best money." I told him it didn't matter to me; I would much rather be doing something I love to do and get paid less than to be waking up every day to go to a job that was sucking the life out of me.

I was perfectly happy with the choice I made; I was going to take this leap of faith!!!

HALF THE MAN I WAS

09 A Leap of Faith

My first interview occurred two days after I had first walked into the fitness center. I had no knowledge of what was about to happen. All I knew for certain was that I wasn't going to take the treatment dished out at that factory. First, I sat and talked with one of the owners, Rick, for about an hour. In the beginning, I'll admit that everything he was saying sounded good, but some of the things he was said had me wondering. He explained how a trainer is paid. I heard that a trainer gets paid "X amount of dollars" for every client that is in the class. What I should have heard was the trainer had to be the one to get that person(s) to sign up for training. In other words, I would have to build up my own clientele. I saw a guy in the middle of the club with 20 people in his class. In my mind, I was thinking, "That guy is getting paid and soon, I would be too". I spent another hour and a half talking to him. He shared some of his story about how he had worked in the construction business before starting at the gym. He explained how he made good money, but it wasn't fulfilling. Although he was paid well, he didn't have any time to enjoy the fruits of his labor. He talked about his father always saying that when he retired, he was going to do so many things. Sadly, his dad was unable to do it because he had to work so long, that life never gave him a chance.

My second interview with Rick went very well also. However, I was about to have a shift in gears in my mindset. He told me that he didn't want me to get wrapped up into having a bunch of clients to train as a personal trainer. He wanted me to think BIGGER. He told me that they wanted to give me my own gym! Now, I was very aware of my surroundings, and noticed a camera in the corner of the room. Suddenly, I was under the impression that I was being "punked" and this conversation was going to be on film. Let me digress and remind you of this incredible timeline of events. I walked in this club and talked to a man about becoming a trainer and was told that they weren't hiring at that time. On the same day, I emailed pictures of my body transformation, along with my resume and links to some newspaper and magazine write ups that had been done about my health journey. And now, I was told that they wanted to give me my own gym one day. I was FLOORED! He explained to me that this company was looking to expand and needed to train more owner/operators. There were other locations and were run by people who first worked for them and now are owners of the clubs. It was just a few days before, which I had made the decision to do something that mattered in life. I had spent considerable time online, looking for ways to get certified to be a personal trainer. The cost just wasn't affordable at all, especially since I had no job. But I do believe that God worked it out for my good and I thank and praise Him for that. Not even a week later, I was in training!

Before I actually began the training, I was asked to come to the corporate office to meet Jason, the President of the company. All I could think was this just got REAL. He apparently was impressed with the way I presented myself and by the end of the meeting, he told me that Rick would get back to me with a job offer. At the next meeting, he quoted a salary that I knew wasn't anywhere near what I was making at the factory. But, truth be told, I would've done it for $50 less; that is just how unhappy I was with my current job. Additionally, I had already given my notice, so something was better than nothing.

The next step was going home and letting my wife know what was on the table for me. I told her the offer and it seemed as if she had a calculator in her head. She did the math so fast, saying something that I hadn't even considered. She told me that the salary offered wasn't going to be enough to cover my half of the bills. And this was before any taxes and other deductions were taken out. We had just put together a budget to make things easier for us to manage. Unfortunately, the amount of money that I would bring home every two weeks was less than what I was bringing home weekly at the other job. I went back and asked if I could possibly get $100.00 more per week in order for me to be able to cover my portion of the bills. He wasn't willing to bend on this issue, stating that if he complied, I would always expect him to do it again. However, he did say that he would pay me for various odd jobs like taking pictures and doing artwork for events at the clubs. Of course, this still didn't make the wife happy. Rick then said he would take a look at giving me more later on down the line.

The training began at the corporate offices. There were five of us. Some were being trained to be a manager at one of the 5 clubs; the rest were being trained to work at the front desk. At this time, I felt like I was getting great information. The instructor/trainer, Michael, was the best when it came down to teaching. He had spent some time as a classroom teacher and knew how to have engaging lessons.

Even though I was extremely optimistic about my new position, life was still very hectic. I still had a few days left to complete my work at the factory. Now, I was away from home from 4 A.M. until 8 P.M. every day for the next two weeks. Needless to say, my wife was upset about this. I was unable to help her with our youngest, getting her from place to place to her after school activities. We had relocated before the end of the school year to another district and wanted our daughter to finish out her eighth grade year where she was enrolled. This made it difficult because of my long schedule. My wife worked the midnight shift and couldn't get much rest running back and forth between towns. All of us were happy when the school year was over.

At the start, I was told that I was going to be placed on the fast track of training and would be working in a club soon. I understood that I had a huge opportunity to earn a great living but it wasn't going to be easy. Rick shared that there were going to be some programs he was going to allow me to take a leadership role and I'd be able to get paid a percentage for being a program leader. This sounded great, however, it could take some considerable time before I would see any real money in order to maintain my household. My initial training lasted a week. At first, I felt like I wasn't ready, but I now know that it was a good thing for me. I'm the type of person who learns better by the "hands-on method", which in the end, worked for my benefit.

The first weeks of working in the gym were rough. The fitness manager, Ridge, was a young guy. This wasn't a surprise to me because I was told that most of the gym operators were young. This was the company's way of growing. They would take young people and show them how to run the business and make them owner/operators. I remember one of my first conversations with him. He explained to me the genius thinking of the owners. The fact that you owned a piece of the club would make you more aware of the club's operations. He made sure that I understood from the beginning that I was in the right place at the right time.

I am so happy that I was given this opportunity after being a part of a network marketing business. This was a time of mindset growth for me. All of the recordings, group calls, presentations, and the books that I read during my networking business phase prepared me for this moment. One of the first things that happened when I got to the club is something that probably goes on in most work environments. A few club members told me that they didn't care for Ridge. They said that they were glad I was there. It's a good thing I didn't take it to heart. I give everyone a chance and I wasn't willing to let the opinions of others shape my own. The truth is he can be a little "OCD" at times, but I love him for it; however there were other times when I didn't understand him.

He had me doing jobs around the club that I just couldn't understand the reason behind them. There was a guy who came in every night at 7pm to clean the facility, but for the first 2 months, Ridge had me cleaning! For the life of me, I didn't comprehend why I was cleaning bathrooms and mopping floors. Now, it all makes sense; he wanted to make sure that I cared about the place as if it was my own. Cleaning the toilets and mopping floors helped me to maintain my humbleness. If you ask me, I think some of the things that he had me do in the beginning was to see if I was a quitter. He'd been so used to people not sticking around. In this case, he had the wrong one. It was going to take more than some dirty toilets to make me walk away.

Not even two weeks later, the fast track training moved even faster. Another gym down the street closed its doors without much warning to its members. Our front door was swinging open and closed so much with new people and here I was a "newbie" myself. Talk about rush hour. This was more like rush month! We learned about the closing days before it happened and hurriedly advertised that we were going to do a special deal for the people who were members of that gym. I was forced to learn a lot of operations very quickly. We did all that we could to make as many of the new members as happy as we could. Hundreds of them flowed in as I was just getting to know the ones that had been here for a while. Nevertheless, we weren't able to make everyone happy, but such is life. Usually, people aren't happy when change is forced upon them and these people had been truly forced. Many people found out about the closing through social media. Some of the older people had learned by seeing a sign on the door. I actually felt a little sorry for them because many had been members for ten years.

One of the hardest things that I had to do at the gym was to get Ridge to understand the fact that I had a wife and a daughter at home. Because he was young, he couldn't understand my family obligations. I understood that this was a great opportunity but at the same time, I had to make sure that I got my daughter to school and her other activities. The only thing he could say was when he started, he sometimes didn't have time to eat. For this reason, I guess he felt like he had to make sure I wasn't given time to do things outside of the club. I had to make sure he understood that my family was important to me as well as my job. Things were hard for us in the beginning, but I'm glad we both were able to get past the rocky period. I think these "growing pains" made our relationship greater and we'll be two of the best leaders in the company one day. I tell him all the time that what he had done as a young man is an awesome accomplishment and that I'm proud of him. There's beauty in the fact that older and younger generations can learn from each other.

In the beginning, this new job took a lot of time away from home and I was getting paid less money. My daily schedule allowed me no free time at all. I was working split shifts, opening everyday, and getting four hours off in the middle of the day, going back for the last four hours of the day. While I was so grateful to FINALLY have a career that I loved, it was casing discord in my personal life. There was a lot of pressure on me; I was doing something that mattered, helping others, but I was unable to help my own family. I tried to explain to my wife how I felt. I knew it was going to be worth it "one day". For her, one day was not good enough. She wanted and needed my help at this present time but I was still in the training process. Many times, I was just overwhelmed. The pressure was building up at home, so I had to ask for a schedule adjustment in order to at least be with my family once a week. I'm extremely grateful that all of the owners were understanding and made it happen. Prayerfully, with the great sales of this book (smile), I'll be able to find that place where I'll have more opportunities to spend quality time with my family, especially since I'm now a "PawPaw".

Personally, over the years I had been working hard with trainers to lose my extra weight, but giving directions to others was a bit challenging. Instructing them on how to run up and down a hill or ride a bike was all I knew. I watched the other trainers lead the group training classes to learn all that I could because I knew that my day was coming soon and it did. When that time came, my spirit was there but my knowledge of how to teach the exercises was not. Luckily for me, nobody was being critical of me and was willing to give me a chance to learn. However, one day, there were two people in the class who were unhappy with me right away. They went to Ridge and right away voiced their opinions. Even now, one of them still won't train with me because of my very first class performance. Do you remember that I told you I had spirit? I was that one who was giving my all to my people; I hadn't learned the difference between coaching and yelling yet. I was in clients' faces, not in a drill sergeant way, but I was loud. The team training is done on the floor, in the middle of the gym, and some of the older members didn't know how to take me at first. They weren't happy with my tone and made complaints to Ridge about me. One of the other fitness manager/owners, Mike, told me that he loved the way I operated and I wasn't going to make everyone happy. He told me not to change who I was because it was what made me special and different from the other trainers. However, Ridge told me to 'take it down a few notches". The way he said it kind of "took the fire out of me" for a moment. I have since found middle ground with my way of training and I think my clients are happy with the way I move them.

During the first few months, Rick took the time to meet with me and talk about how things were progressing. There were a few concepts that, in the beginning, I wasn't too sure about but I wasn't going to let anything get in the way of the great opportunity that had been given to me. I now had several opportunities to make extra money to supplement my salary. While working at the gym, I still had other "irons in the fire". During the first few meetings, I shared them with Rick, i.e., the photography, graphics designs, network marketing, and my ministry at the church. Lastly, let's not forget the fact that I was in the process of writing a book...(Wink)

As a businessman concerned only about the growth of the gym, I think that my other interests stayed on his mind. I'm assuming he wondered about my full commitment to the gym. I say this because at one meeting, he wrote down everything I was doing and made sure that I understood what was important to him. I explained to him that I wouldn't let these things get in the way of my learning how to run the club. I also made it clear to him that there were two things that I was not going to stop doing and that was church ministry and writing this book.

Even though I've owned businesses in past years, learning the nature of a gym was a larger beast. I have second-guessed some things in life before. It wasn't even 3 months after I started working when the Ridge brought in one of his childhood friends. In the beginning, I wasn't sure how everything would play out. In my mind, I was thinking that since this was his friend, I wouldn't be able to say anything to him. So I just sat back and watched. The friend had a different outlook on what the company was moving to do. But the goal of the company was to make all of us leaders and one day, owner-operators of our own gyms. However, all he wanted to do was to be a trainer. He was good at what he did and was great with the people he worked with, but this was not the plan and he was doing everything differently from the way I was being shown. He did not understand the overall goal of the company was to make us owner/operators. Or that it would take some time to work his way up to the next level. It took me some time to understand that Ridge was about his business and even though this was his friend he was going to do what was right for his business. I was sure that I was going to be replaced and that his buddy was going to take my place. This just shows that I hadn't matured in the business aspect of working at the corporate level. I soon found out that everything was on the "up and up" as I was told it would be. I pulled ridge to the side and told him that I didn't feel that my position was secure. He made it very clear that I was his partner and I had nothing to worry about. It turned out that his friend wasn't ready for this opportunity and even though he was being groomed to have the opportunity to run his own club, he put in his notice and returned back to his hometown.

There comes a time in life where you'll have to learn how to show a person ways to make fitness and health a part of their budget. The truth is if they aren't ready, they will still find a way to tell you how they can't afford to take better care of themselves. Usually, I'm thinking, how can they not believe this? I'll be honest this wasn't always my mindset. You have to catch a person at the right time. Yet others, like myself, had the eye-opening experience of having a doctor say it's a life or death situation if the weight doesn't come off.

Let me share another story with you. We, unlike many gyms, provide a service to help people get off of the right foot from the very start. Every member that gets a membership at the club gets a free fitness assessment. Without going into all of the details of a potential client's financial history, we go through areas where he or she could "cut back" on some expenses in order to be able to afford a training plan. It may be the extreme cost of cigarettes or daily cups of Starbucks coffee, for example. During a service session with a member, she told me that she had taken a look at her credit card statement and had spent over $300 dining out during the month with 10 days left to go. She also expressed how she drank a $20 bottle of wine weekly, sometimes two. By the time we were done adding all of her monthly expenditures that weren't helping her weight loss goal, the total came to approximately $450. I took her on the floor to perform a very simple functional movement test. She was floored by the fact that she couldn't perform most of the test. I could see the tears in her eyes. But I told her how I had a plan to help her. This included the coaching and accountability she needed to help her on her journey to a healthier lifestyle. I offered her structured classes that would remove all of the guessing; all she had to do was show up. She would receive a coach for every session. Also included was a meal plan to get her on the right track. Additionally, she would be able to meet with me once a month for guidance and have a half hour accountability session. What is the moral of this story? One can point out ways to help people who hurt inside, begging for help but the truth is, until they are truly ready for a lifestyle change, it won't happen.

In May 2016, the gym owners told me about a program that the supplement company that we promoted was always looking for a "spokesperson athlete." This would be equivalent to a "poster child" for the March of Dimes, let's say. I thought they were kidding. I wasn't even close to being an athlete! Surely, I had done something great by losing the large amount of weight, but I didn't think anyone would consider me an athlete. So it was time for me to take my training to the next level; I needed something more than a meal replacement to build muscle. I submitted the forms and on June 2016, I became a sponsored athlete for a supplement company, Dotfit. Fortunately, that company was willing to support me. I was now on the next phase of my personal health journey. At the time of this writing, I'm just getting started but I am beginning to feel the results already. Perhaps I'll include more about this in my next book.

By late June, the company began to have leadership meetings with a group of five of us. These were the next set of leaders that would be taught to run the newly opened clubs. I was very happy to be chosen for this opportunity. Now, I would learn all of the business operations. It's amazing how life can change in the blink of an eye! I walked into a club with hopes of being able to use my story to help other people achieve optimum health and now, I was put into a position to learn how to run my own club. God had placed me in the right place at the right time. This training opened my eyes to learn more about myself. I needed to keep my ego "in check". In the beginning, I was so fast to point my finger at others. I was unable to see that with position, I had been given a lot of responsibility and if things didn't go the way it should, I had to take ownership for it. The leaders of this company wouldn't allow me to place blame on others. There are five levels of leadership as explained by one of the greatest leaders in the world, John C. Maxwell. I had to get to the next level in order to grow my "leadership lid." Leaders can't make other leaders if they are at the top of the mountain by themselves.

Before I come to the end of my story, I want to mention about one last thing. I have been motivating people for many years about moving in the right direction with their weight loss goals by introducing them to meal replacements, physical workouts, or by simply sharing my story over social media. When I started at the gym I was sure that I would have some of my friends and family become a part of what I was doing. In the beginning, I reached out to as many as I could, to do just that. Unfortunately, I was unable to get anyone to come over to the club to check it out. The truth was, I had all I needed right there in the club. My family's unwillingness to support me hurt the most. I expressed these feelings to a deacon friend and he pulled me aside to tell me that I inspire many people; my story was going to help so many people. He made sure I understood that my family and friends would be the last to come around and all I had to do was keep doing what I was doing and everything was going to be alright.

Not even two weeks later I had a checkpoint with one of my clients. All clients who are in a service with the gym get a checkpoint once a month to sit down with me or the other fitness manager to talk about their progress. Some may have not reached them, so we look at their food logs and check fitness class attendance. As I was talking with her, she told me how someone had told her that I "didn't really care about some people". I was truly confused at first, but as she went on, it was clear to me that this was starting to become a racial issue. I asked her if she felt this way. She told me that she didn't have a problem with what I was doing and that I was there for her just like anyone else. I'm the kind of person that doesn't look at life in black and white. I truly believe that there is only one race on this earth and that is the human race.

HALF THE MAN I WAS

10 The Wrap-Up

As this part of my story comes to a close, my mind goes back to the beginning behavior of overeating. As previously stated, many times, it begins at childhood. Most people, especially parents, believe that children will be able to burn off the calories from excessive eating because their metabolism is high. But the truth is, these children may be on their way to become overweight adults. Childhood obesity is REAL! According to the CDC (Centers for Disease Control and Prevention), childhood obesity has more than doubled in children and quadrupled in adolescents in the past 30 years. Obese youth are more likely to have risk factors for cardiovascular disease, such as high cholesterol or high blood pressure. In a population-based sample of children ranging from ages 5-17 years old, 70% of obese youth had at least one risk factor for cardiovascular disease. Furthermore, children and adolescents who are obese are at greater risk for bone and joint problems, sleep apnea, and social and psychological problems such as poor self-esteem.

During the summer months of my childhood, my friends and I "toured" the city, taking advantage of the free lunch program. We rode our bikes every day, visiting 2-3 schools. However, that number went up on pizza days. We'd hit all 6 schools on that special day of the week! I never gave any thought that this experience would catch up with me. Thinking back, those pizza "slices" were probably not a recommended serving size. As I recall, they were pretty big. Moreover, pizza wasn't the only food item on the tray. We were eating what 6 people would have eaten…all in a day, not to mention dinner later that evening.

Unfortunately, many parents unknowingly are setting their children up for a pathway to living an unhealthy lifestyle. However, today's food prices play an important role in this behavior. It is SO much cheaper to feed a family with "fast" foods than with healthier choices. Restaurant chains encourage this habit by offering "dollar menus" filled with burgers, French fries, and deep-fried chicken strips. Many gas stations now sell pizza, hot dogs, chips, ice cream, and other calorie-loaded foods. Gone are the days when meals were prepared and families sat down to eat together. Our fast-paced society doesn't have time, or better yet, make the time to simply eat to live and not live to eat.

I can only hope that some of the stories in this book will make you think a bit more about the food choices you make for yourself and your family. I have spent the last two years working on this book, my story, not because I wanted pats on the back or fame and fortune. As I've stated before, I truly believe that my mission in life is to help others. If the people who I come in contact with can learn from my mistakes and experiences, then my mission is complete. However, this charge is on going. I will continue to share my story as long as there is breath in my body. Throughout this journey, I have had highs and lows, but it was predestined in order for me to become the man I am today.

So many incidents and situations prevented me from consistently writing this book. It seems to me that there were various people who didn't want to see me get it done, whether it was my family, friends, or jobs. However, I truly believe that it was meant to happen this way. Many times, I was my worst "enemy". There were periods when I should have made this book a priority, but I chose to do other things. In hindsight, I suppose this was the way it was supposed to be. There were times when others seemed not to believe in me which motivated me all the more. Sometimes doubt, and even hatred can be used as motivational tools. I believe I used doubt to fuel my passion.

Many people have expressed to me that I have lost enough weight. However, I don't agree and will continue working my program until I get to my goal. The truth is, I don't really know exactly what my goal is, but I would like to be able to say that I have lost 300 pounds…just once. It may or may not happen, but I'll keep trying. I just think it would be a cool thing to say. It's that "WOW" factor. But honestly, it's more about the way I look; I want to replace some of the loose skin with lean muscle. Although, I've been blessed not to have so much looseness where it would be mandatory to have surgery to remove that much skin.

Before ending this book, I want to share a few more things. Many people talk about the mentors in their lives who have helped shape their beliefs and character. There were definitely some great ones such as Tony Robbins, Eric Thomas, Les Brown, and John C. Maxwell who my "up close and personal" mentors suggested that I investigate. I refer to these personal mentors as "the three wise bald-headed men". The first one is Vince Adams, who I met and spent considerable time with building my network marketing business. He coached me to help break the fear of public speaking and to understand how powerful my story was. During events, he repeatedly placed me in front of people to address. At the "drop of a hat", I might add. I LOVE to talk and have never been shy around small groups of people. Posting pictures and little anecdotes was easy, but speaking in a room filled with hundreds of people was quite a different story. In the beginning, Vince made sure that I understood the power of positive thinking. He taught me how to set and write down goals. I still have many goals written in notebooks that I am able to look back and say, "Yes, I reached that one!" What a great feeling! I already have some goals set for 2017 and am so happy that Vince taught me the power of affirmations and positive thinking.

My next bald-headed mentor was my personal trainer, Kris Kalmese. As mentioned before, he started working with me after I had initially lost over 180 pounds. We definitely had different ways of thinking, but were able to grow in a way that was great for both of us. He made sure that I understood that I myself was a "product" and with my story, I would be able to share my story to inspire others on their journeys. During my time with Kris, I was always amazed that I could actually perform exercises I once thought impossible like hanging upside down on gymnastic rings. Certainly, that was a feat designed only for skinny people! He always pushed me to my limits and never allowed me to make excuses. But what I'm MOST grateful for is he opened my eyes to the wonderful world of healthy food choices. Thanks to this man, I am now able to take $20 and turn it into meals that last a full week.

The last of the three wise bald-headed men is Mike Orwig, who is one of the gym owners. Millions of people have jobs that give them no sense of self-fulfillment, but not in my case. I'm able to share my journey with people who need it most. I must say this about Mike. I don't believe that no one will ever meet a man who is so compassionate about helping others. His earlier career as an educator allowed him to develop a unique teaching style that can have any person do whatever it takes to reach his or her goals, not only in weight loss, but life. His ability to remain positive, no matter what the situation, has taken me to a higher level of thinking. Although I've only worked with him for a little over six months, I'm sure he will always be someone that I can count on to keep me on the right track.

It's no secret that the news and social media keep us aware of what's happening in the world and in the areas where we live. Because of this, many people are always upset with me because I refuse to start my day with negative things. The truth is, I stay as far away as I can from constantly "staying in the know", whether it's on the local or worldwide level. Yes, there are some things a person should be aware of but to live in fear is just crazy to me. I use my media outlets differently. YouTube is the first thing I tune in to every morning. There are so many channels available to get started off with the right mindset; my choice is motivational videos. The way one begins his or her day can help set a positive state of mind. Over the years, I've definitely listened to or watched programs/movies that had me feeling just the opposite. However, with what I choose to penetrate my brain now, helps me to stay positive and not allow pessimism to control my emotions.

Over the last few years, I've learned to be more creative in my thinking, thus consuming foods that are healing to my body. Don't get me wrong, taste is VERY important and I can just about make anything taste as good as any fast food establishment. The secret to this lies in the seasonings used. There are many varieties available that are packed with flavor without the salt. For example, I'm in LOVE with cheese, but not with the effects of what it does to my body. There is just so much fat in it. Consequently, I've learned to use nutritional yeast to get that same cheesy flavor minus the fat. The next thing that I do is a substitute oven-baked parsnip fries to get over my addiction to deep fried potatoes. I believe that French fries are one of the most addictive foods for millions of people. It's no wonder that that famous restaurant with the "golden arches" sell so many! And man, don't let them come right out of that hot oil! Before your mouth begins to salivate and you make a run to get those fries, let me help you better understand why they are so addictive. Craving fried and oily foods can indicate a simple essential fatty acid deficiency. Try eating more quality fats such as chia seeds, dark chocolate, avocados, and fatty fish such as salmon, tuna, and trout. Just be careful not to overdo it. Too much of any food is not good either; portion control is key. Also, fries contain starch and salt. When the body craves starch, it has trouble maintaining a stable blood sugar level to keep the right amount of sugar in your bloodstream. Cravings for salt are usually associated with high stress levels. Some experts say that taking a hot bath, getting a massage, or just simply letting the beauty of the world sink in, can sometimes satisfy cravings. If you have strong cravings for certain foods, please research the triggers. There's a wealth of information from credible websites available.

Lastly, I want to warn you about adding condiments such as ketchup and other sauces to your food. Many of them contain large doses of extra fats, sodium, and calories. For example, just two tablespoons of mayonnaise can add 200 calories and 24 grams of fat to whatever you're eating. Furthermore, it has NO nutritional value. I once read that a half-cup of some brands of syrup may contain up to 438 calories and 107 grams of sugar. Look up the nutritional facts of what you eat and learn to substitute ingredients to suit your taste buds. Your heart and body will thank you for it. Oh, I almost forgot! I'm including my very own recipe for homemade oven-baked kale chips. Kale is loaded with all sorts of beneficial compound, some of which have powerful medicinal properties. Take a chance; you may love them as much as I do.

Over the years, I have learned that you can't expect the people in your life to follow suit with your health journey. The most difficult group to reach are usually the ones who are the closest to you. A conscience change has to be made by each individual person. For years, I made New Year's resolutions and goals to lose weight, only to return to my bad eating habits. Maybe these resolutions should be renamed "New Life" resolutions. Getting and staying must be more than a 90-day commitment. I've faced many challenges over my life and I know there will be many more. Regardless, I'm very fortunate to share my story with you. There are so many more things that I want to share, but maybe it would be better on the "big screen". I'd love to have a movie depicting my life story. But until then...my acknowledgments...

Lastly, I would like to thank the people who helped me with this entire process of putting my words in print. As I stated previously, this book has been an ongoing development for the past two years of my life. First and foremost, I'd like to thank my wife, Carla, and my family for putting up with me through this "adventure". It's been a long haul, but WE MADE IT!

I owe a debt of gratitude to **Quinn Riley**, a classmate and published author, who has been following my weight loss journey over the years. He was able to help me understand the power of my story, making sure that I shared the "good, bad, and ugly" of it all.

Many thanks are due to my editor, **Debra Davis Humble**, who happens to be my former 8th grade English teacher. She played a huge part in helping make sense of my story so that you, the reader, would understand it. It's funny to me that I had a huge crush on her back then. I should have paid more attention in class so she wouldn't have had to work so hard.

Recipes
Marlowe's Cheesy Garlic Kale Chips

Over the years, I've been able to "throw" together (or create, if you will) a few special recipes of my own. I'm only sharing one creation to show you how easy it is to start putting ingredients together for tasty main dishes, salads, or snacks. There may come a time when you'll be purchasing my very own healthy choices cookbook. I've gotten ideas from recipes that I've seen online; my favorite site is Pinterest. Sometimes, all you may need to do is just reach into your own cabinets. You'd be surprised to see what you can come up with.

Remember those kale chips that my daughter now loves? Take a chance and follow the recipe below; you may find that it will become your new favorite "go-to" snack. Please note that I didn't specify the amount of seasonings. Use your discretion and season the kale to your taste.

 1-2 bunch(es) of freshly washed kale
 olive or coconut oil
 nutritional yeast
 garlic powder
 cumin
 roasted sesame seeds
 black pepper
 ground sunflower seeds
 Cajun spice (for extra "heat") OPTIONAL

1. Remove the stems from the kale before rinsing.

2. After rinsing, lightly pat dry. (You may want to coat the kale with oil and add the seasonings in a big bowl. Or, just skip to the next step.)

3. Lightly coat the kale with the oil of your choice. Don't overdo it; it adds fat. (Cooking sprays will work, but beware of the chemicals added.)

4. Thoroughly mix all of the dry seasonings together in a bowl.

5. Spread the kale on a baking sheet or pan. You may want to line the sheet with foil and lightly spray to prevent sticking.

6. Sprinkle the seasoning mix and cover the kale to your taste.

7. Bake approximately 15 minutes in a preheated oven at 250 degrees. Remember that some ovens cook faster than others. There is a difference in cooking with gas or with electric stoves.

8. ENJOY!

RECIPES

HALF THE MAN I WAS

One Last Thing

I want to leave you with an example of what I may eat in a 24-hour period. This is just a guideline of what works for me when I'm on track to hit my personal weight loss goal. First of all, logging your food intake is extremely important. It's so easy to remember that you had oatmeal, an apple, and a cup of coffee for breakfast. Perhaps you had a protein bar as a mid morning snack and a small salad and tuna for lunch. What you may not remember are the two miniature candy bars you swiped from a coworker's desk. Or that bag of potato chips from the vending machine just to "hold you over" until dinnertime. All of these extra food items contain not only extra calories, but also fats, carbs, and proteins. Logging your food will help you keep track of the amount of these macronutrients.

In order to stay on track, I feel it is very important to meal prep. There are many ways to do this. Some people prep for their daily lunches only, while others meal prep for every meal during the week. Nothing goes in my mouth without it being weighed, counted or scanned into my food-logging app. My best results are when I follow a plan with 150 grams of carbs, 200 grams of protein, and 35-40 grams of fat. You must find what works best for your body.

I've been asked many times about what a typical day is like for me, so here goes…After my morning protein shake, I take off for the gym, making sure that I have had some type of carbs, 25-35 grams, to power me through my workout. Remember, carbs are where we get our energy. After my workout, I have a nice breakfast with 2-3 eggs with spinach and a grain cereal with fiber. Be aware that individuals have different goals in mind, whether it is to shed pounds by losing weight or to build lean muscle.

My next meal is where I take the time to actually cook. Usually, I'll prepare a piece of lean meat such as fish or chicken with some vegetables. Most of the time, I use a mixed medley such as broccoli, cauliflower, and carrots. There are many frozen varieties in the local grocery stores, so feel free to experiment. I can put together a meal in less than 25 minutes. Most lean meats aren't thick so it doesn't take long to get done. If time is limited, there is nothing wrong with lightly oiling a skillet with olive or coconut oil to pan fry the meat in 15 minutes or less. Remember to pay close attention to the serving size recommendations on the packaging of foods, along with the carbs, protein, etc. Some of the best low-carb vegetables are broccoli, bell peppers, asparagus, zucchini, and cauliflower, to name a few. As always, be aware of the amount of salt and butter used when preparing any food.

If I get hungry before dinner, I sometimes make another meal replacement shake or eat a protein bar. In most cases, I almost always have some type of healthy snack option with me. My dinners are about the same as my lunch, lean meat with veggies. However, I try to stay away from having too many carbs before bedtime. I like to have dinner between 5:00 and 6:00 in the evening, and end my day with a protein shake right before going to sleep. At 4:00 A.M., it's time to start my day all over again. So there, you have it, a day of dining with me.

Best wishes to you as you venture into your new healthy lifestyle.

ONE LAST THING

HALF THE MAN I WAS

"SERENITY PRAYER"
- Reinhold Niebuhr (1892-1971)

God grant me the serenity

To accept the things I cannot change;

Courage to change the things I can;

And the wisdom to know the difference.

Living one day at a time; enjoying one moment at a time;

Accepting hardships as the pathway to peace;

Taking, as He did, this sinful world as it is.

Not as I would have it;

Trusting that He will make all things right

If I surrender to His Will;

That I may be reasonably happy in this life

And supremely happy with Him

Forever in the next.

AMEN.

HALF THE MAN I WAS

HALF THE MAN I WAS

Acknowledgments

First and foremost, I thank God for allowing me the chance to share my story. Throughout the years of this journey, my family has had to take a "back seat", especially in the last few months. I owe huge thanks to my wonderful wife, Carla and teenaged daughter, Tyleah. These two had to deal with me not being there when they needed me. I hope now, since this is finished, they understand that all I wanted was to get the message out to people who needed to hear this story.

I also want to thank the two people who brought me into this world, my mother, Patricia Whitlow, who loves me with all her heart, no matter what. She pushed me on with a "never quit" attitude. Also, thanks to my father, Alvin Scott, whose charm I was "blessed" to inherit. His belief that he is the finest man in the world drove me to believe the same thing, no matter how big I was.

Many thanks to Keisha Randle Smith, Lucinda Steinke, Shelly Link, and Jeff Nogoda for taking the time to read the book as part of the review team. They were able to catch things missed by using fresh eyes. I also have to thank the countless friends, family and followers on my social media sites. Their feedback, over the years, has been extremely helpful; not only the people who cheered me on during my transformation, but also the ones who did not believe that I could do it.

Finally, thanks to the two people who stuck with me from the beginning to the end of this book journey. My chief editor, Debra Davis Humble had the hardest job. She sat with me, correcting all of my errors and believe me, there were many.

We spent this past year writing and rewriting, making sure that my story would be easy to follow, even when I sometimes wrote and rambled in circles. Through the losses of friends and family and her illnesses, she didn't turn her back on me and continued to help me on this first project of many. I love her for all that she has done and how she made sure that this book could be the best it could be.

Lastly, huge thanks go out to the man, my classmate, Quinn Scott Riley, who birthed the seed in me to share my story. I thank him for taking interest and helping me to shape the outline of this book. I will have to admit that at first, when he told me to share some of the things from my past, I didn't understand how they would all play into the story, but he was right. Everything was very important to make this book more than about one man's weight loss journey but how these events shaped him (me) to be a better person. Not only to help myself, but to help others around me. I know that there are so many things that were left out of this story but, it's like Quinn said, "Bruh man, Some things are meant for the big screen."

Special Credits and Thank You

Thanks to my photographer, Wayne Baranowski at Wayba Productions. Your shots really worked well for the website and book art.

Thanks to my Web designer, Ricky White Designs/BlackEagle Marketing. You really laid out my vision of what I wanted the site to look like, clean and professional.

Also, thanks to the Sean Hicks of Gargoyle Creative who was able to take my vision and bring it to life with an impressive book cover and back page layout.

Lastly, I have to thank my Morning Star Church family who lifted my family up with their monetary gifts when we were at our darkest hour. Special thanks for the continued support of my cousins/friends, Rico and Alvita Calhoun. They stayed beside us and never passed judgment and always encouraged us with open arms.

About the Author

Marlowe Whitlow is the epitome of the title of this book, Half The Man he was, Through trials and tribulations, countless diet plans, and eventually hard work (outs) and determination, he was able to lose over half of his body weight which was just shy of 500 pounds. His positive attitude and never-ending drive has helped to change the lives of countless people in his community and around the country.

After years of sharing his story, he was convinced by a longtime friend and classmate to write a book about his life's journey. Marlowe, holding nothing back, from being a drug dealer to his brush with death, is open and honest about his past, which directly relates to his present and future.

Currently, as a certified personal trainer and a gym manager, he mentors people in showing how they can live longer healthier lives. This book will make the reader think about making better food, and possibly better life choices in order to be and stay healthy.

Made in the USA
Middletown, DE
28 January 2017